5
STEPS
TO SUCCESSFUL
MONEY
MANAGEMENT

How to Live Wisely and Worry Less

5 STEPS TO SUCCESSFUL MONEY MANAGEMENT

LEE E. DAVIS

How to Live Wisely and Worry Less

BROADMAN PRESS
NASHVILLE, TENNESSEE

© Copyright 1993 ● Broadman Press

All rights reserved

4253-56

ISBN: 0-8054-5356-3

Dewey Decimal Classification: 332.024

Subject Headings: FINANCE, PERSONAL // BUDGETS, HOUSEHOLD //
STEWARDSHIP

Library of Congress Card Catalog Number: 92-26089

Printed in the United States of America

Unless otherwise stated, all Scripture quotations are from the *King James Version of the Bible.*

Scripture quotations marked NASB are from the *New American Standard Bible.* © The Lockman Foundation, 1960, 1962, 1963, 1968, 1971, 1972, 1973, 1975, 1977. Used by permission.

Library of Congress Cataloging-in-Publication Data

Davis, Lee E., 1938-

Five steps to successful money management / Lee E. Davis

p. cm.

ISBN: 0-8054-5356-3

1. Finance, Personal—United States. 2. Budgets, Personal—United States.
3.Saving and thrift—United States. 4. Investments—United States. I. Title.

HG179.D348   1993

332.024—dc20   92-26089

CIP

In Appreciation

Many, many people have contributed to the contents of this book through their participation and fellowship in conferences I've led. I am thankful for all of you who encouraged me, challenged me, and helped enrich my understanding of stewardship and money management.

I'm also deeply grateful to my colleagues at the SBC Stewardship Commission and to the state stewardship/ Cooperative Program directors and associates. Your gifts of wisdom are reflected in all that I do.

Among my colleagues of recent years, one was a unique friend and teacher. With great appreciation I remember the late John C. Ivins of Virginia.

Lee E. Davis

Forms, Graphs, and Lists

Contents

INTRODUCTION

**In This Book
You Can Learn How to**

- Keep from worrying about your bank balance.
- Be more contented.
- Have a happier family.
- Stop paying interest to other people.
- Make your money work for you.
- Pay cash for your cars.
- Have money to give away.
- Have an adequate retirement income.

Why should you and I manage our money with care and for maximum benefit anyway? The majority of people don't. A prevalent attitude was expressed by a person who said to me, "Living on my income is below my dignity." That's another way of saying, "I deserve more and better than I can afford." There are many casualties among people of this ilk. I know, because I was one of them for 21 years.

There's a question circulating which asks, "What do you get when you play a country-western song backwards?" The answer: "You get your wife back; you get your job back; you get your house back; and you get your truck back."

It might be nice if we could "play our life backwards" and correct some of the financial mistakes we've made over the years. We can't, but I've discovered that a person or family can start where they are and make wise financial decisions for the future. The mistakes of the past can't be changed, but they can be tempered.

The Decision That Changed Our Lives

A pop song asks, "How can a loser ever win?" We had been losers in money management, but when I was about age 40, my wife, Sarah, and I decided to change our losing ways. We had been on a financial merry-go-round. But unlike a merry-go-round at a carnival where an operator stops the wheel for people to get on and off, no one outside can stop a person or family from mismanaging money. It's an internal decision which only those involved can do anything about.

This book outlines and illustrates what we did—the principles we applied and the system we used—how a loser can, in fact, become a winner. I know these principles and this system will work for any person or family who has a livable income and who will make the effort. You don't have to win a sweepstakes to accomplish what we have accomplished in the past 13 years. But you've got to want to change enough to make some difficult choices.

At first we chose to forego some immediate gratifications in favor of more meaningful long-range successes.

Consider some of the benefits you can enjoy as the result of wise, conscientious money management.

Contrasting our financial condition now to the past, we are never without cash. We still watch our checking account balance, but it's to keep from accumulating too much money in a low interest-bearing account. We have no installment payments on bank consolidation loans or credit cards. We have the suggested amount of emergency funds. We have paid cash for all of our cars since starting our new money management plan more than 10 years ago. Our retirement plans are in place and adequately funded for a comfortable retirement lifestyle. And we have a more courageous faith, and can give more money for ministries than we ever thought was possible.

The secret we discovered for improving our finances and reaching our goals was getting money to work for us rather than just working for money. We started by carefully budgeting our money. With a budget we directed our spending, eliminated interest payments, and increased our cash flow.

Next, we started investing our money. In just over a decade we have gone from a negative net worth to income from investments which will soon compare with earned income, and much of it is tax sheltered. We physically handle very little of this investment income because it's automatically reinvested. The reinvested interest and dividends compound earnings in subsequent months and years. In time, our money will produce more income than we can earn by working.

"We can't afford it" is a statement we don't make anymore, not that we have money to buy any luxury a person could want. Rather, we have goals, and it's our goals which guide most of our spending. Being able to afford something is not the issue; reaching our goals is what is important.

> The ingredients of wise and successful money management are time and money. The more time you have the less money is needed to accomplish your goals. Start young, grow in faith, work hard, manage wisely, and enjoy the benefits.

A Past We'll Never Forget

Until we resolved to manage money more wisely, our finances were in shambles. For 21 years we survived financially on credit. We didn't live from one paycheck to the next; that implies living within the limits of our income. We spent more than our incomes. Each year we went deeper into debt. Ironically, we accumulated more debt as the result of increases in income. We could afford larger payments. At the time we decided to change, it was taking about 40 percent of our spendable income just to make monthly payments on a bank consolidation loan and credit cards. Sarah and I lived in agony and fear—agony over the possibility of not being able to provide the necessities for our family, and fear that an emergency would cause our friends to find out that we were more than broke.

Our solution for many years was to do what any decent Christian family would do. We kept our plight hidden. We made every effort to fit in with the times and the occasions. On Easter mom and the girls had new outfits; dad and son had new suits or new accessories. At Christmastime we decorated the house and surrounded the tree with gifts the same as did our friends. We were very much the typical family doing the typical things at the appointed times, all on credit. Not even our children knew about our credit merry-go-round.

Our unstated goal was to avoid financial collapse. We managed our money much as an amateur plate-spinner tries to keep several plates spinning on sticks. We ran from one financial crisis to another trying to keep each one from breaking our money-juggling act.

This is the price we paid for careless money management. Because of the use of credit, the buying power of our income was reduced. Mismanagement also diminished hope because saving money for better days in the future was out of the question.

The emotional price was greater still—worry over providing necessities such as food, clothing, housing, medical care, and transportation dominated our thinking. Not much mental energy was left for creativity since it was mostly depleted thinking about money problems. The emotional strain often spilled over and caused fractured family relationships and reduced effectiveness at work. Closely related to other emotions was our spiritual stability. Feeling like a failure financially sometimes breached a once-courageous faith. A timid faith further confirmed our sense of hopelessness.

Figuratively speaking, we wore masks in public to cover the agony we privately endured. We proved that the proverb is right: "The rich rules over the poor, and the borrower becomes the lender's slave" (Prov. 22:7,

NASB). We felt like slaves. We often struggled to hold on to our faith, which included giving regularly. But our giving was mostly joyless and legalistic, only giving what we thought to be the minimum amount required.

It's difficult to imagine now that just 13 years ago we seldom had cash in our pockets, or in the bank either. We lived on credit and had a minus net worth. (If we had sold everything, we could not have repaid all we owed.) We had no savings or money for emergencies. Retirement plans were woefully inadequate. We were never able to give spontaneously to any person or cause. We fit the description of financial illiterates and emotional cripples.

You Can Improve Your Finances As We Did!

Comparing the before and after of my family's finances, with which do you identify? If given a choice, you surely would choose our new and improved financial condition.

Rick and Deb Sanders are a young couple who had greatly over-extended their credit, mostly with credit cards and car loans. We determined that their minimum monthly payments required between 50 and 60 percent of their spendable income. To their credit, they were fed up with the pressure caused by their money problems, and were willing to do whatever was necessary to improve their financial health.

After sizing up their income and expenses and exploring some options, they decided to sell most everything of value, including two almost-new cars. They agreed with each other to temporarily do without the things that were not essential and replace necessary items, such as the cars, with used and less expensive ones. This included moving to a less expensive apartment. Their goal was to stop using consumer credit and eliminate all debt within two years. (They first suggested a time-frame of one year, but because of the amount of their indebtedness I encouraged them to be more realistic.) Six months later I received word from them through a mutual acquaintance. They had accelerated the plan we worked out and projected that in three more months they would be debt free.

You may not be able to achieve such dramatic results as quickly in your money management as did Rick and Deb, because they had a slightly above-average income. But you can be equally successful if you have the determination of this couple. One's attitude is crucial in effectively solving money problems.

A majority of people can significantly increase their buying power and net worth in a short time without additional income through wiser money management. Why did I change my money management habits? Why did the Sanderses succeed so quickly? We both were tired of being broke and hated the pressure being broke placed on us. I was also disgusted with my lack of discipline and recognized how pitiful were my excuses for living on credit.

If you're having similar feelings, then resolve right now to do whatever is necessary to change and improve your financial strength. As so many people have found who have used these principles and this system, you probably have more money to work with than you think. I'm committed to doing all I can to help you be a successful money manager. But I can't do it for you. It's up to you!

Become what you were made to be. All people are created equal; we're all created as managers (Gen. 1:26-28). In fact, being a manager is not an option; we're either good managers or poor managers. When born, we're given innate intelligence and survival instincts. With these endowments, we're capable of interpreting our environment and acquiring social and work skills which are necessary to exist. Further, we're endowed with a native attribute which gives us a sense of accountability to God. We're responsible for managing life, influence, and resources which we have been provided.

We are stewards. A steward is a person who is manager of something that belongs to someone else. Since we haven't created anything, we're just managing it for the One who did create it. Management is a responsibility, and unlike mismanagement it provides rich dividends. We can curse the darkness or light a candle; we can lament the agonies of mismanagement or seize the contentment found when we manage our money wisely.

In the Starting Blocks

It was a boyhood dream. While I worked in the hot fields of Alabama summers, I was cooled by the imaginary winds that surrounded me. As a thirteen-year-old boy, I could mentally transport myself from a sweltering cotton patch to a cross-country cruise on a motorcycle. It started out as a dream, but soon became a fixed goal when I was fourteen. I wanted a motorcycle. Why? I don't know, except that motorcycles fascinated me, and they probably represented a kind of freedom typical of adolescent cravings.

I challenged myself to do whatever was necessary to own a motorcycle. At age 15, overcoming Dad's mulish resistance and a near insurmountable lack of money, I at last had the object of my goal—a brand new BSA Bantam motorcycle, 400 CCs.

To live with purpose is to have goals. Goals keep us focused, alive, motivated, active, and resilient. If a dirt-poor farm boy could earn and save almost $500 in 1953 to reach a fantasy goal, most people these days shouldn't have much of a problem achieving more practical goals.

Step 1: Establish Your Goals

How important are clearly defined and written goals? A study was done of Yale University alumni. Three percent of the alumni had written goals at the time of graduation. It was found that the goal-setters were worth more financially than the remaining 97 percent combined.[1] What an impressive report, and it compares favorably to my own experience with goal-setting!

Thirteen years have passed since Sarah and I first developed our financial goals. Some of them were extremely ambitious and challenging in light of our financial condition at the time. Yet, we have accomplished all but one of our goals either before planned or by the time projected. The one long-range goal not yet attained is eight or nine years ahead of original plans.

Goals That Worked for My Family

Of course, we have had other goals since the first ones that started us on our money management pilgrimage. But we have accomplished most of our subsequent goals without much fanfare. However, our first goals were more inclusive and were probably more meaningful than later goals. Those first goals best illustrate the value of choosing and pursuing financial goals for spending, saving, and giving.

Goals are usually more easily defined when divided into categories. We separated our goals into three categories:

- Short-range goals—one year
- Medium-range goals—up to five years

• Long-range goals—twenty years or more
I hope you will benefit from some of our experiences.

Goals for Next Year

Our first-year goals included some that were urgent, such as bringing installment debt under control. Other first-year goals merely needed to be launched; for example, beginning volunteer mission work. As I discuss our goals and the money management strategies we used, determine if similar strategies would benefit you and/or your family.

• **Reduce installment debt.**—For more than 20 years of marriage, my wife and I had financed our life-style with department-store and bank-credit cards and consolidation loans. We often used a "robbing-Peter-to-pay-Paul" approach to juggle our debt load. We had no idea what we had bought with the bulk of the money we owed. Even remembering those days of mismanagement is depressing.

Goals have little meaning unless a time-frame is assigned to them. We scheduled a three-year period for our goal of reducing installment debt. In fact, our overriding goal was to get out of debt in three years, except for the house mortgage. Eliminating debt was top priority for us. Such a huge chunk of my income was needed to make monthly payments that significant money growth was impossible until the debt was eliminated.

For several years we quit using credit cards for personal purchases. Any extra or unexpected money we received was used to reduce our debt balance. It's amazing what a financially deprived family can do when committed to a meaningful goal. In two years and seven months we paid off our installment debts! With our debts paid, our buying power increased about 18 percent on that portion of my income which had been used to repay the debt. This was our first major accomplishment. Paying off our debts freed up money which we used to fund our highest-priority goals. Our growth process was under way.

If one of your goals is to eliminate installment debt, I have a few suggestions. Avoid using a consolidation loan, if at all possible. A consolidation loan seems to be the first solution considered by most people with overextended debt. They immediately want to reduce the pain caused by high monthly payments. However, a consolidation loan to deal with debt-overload is seldom the best solution. When monthly payments are reduced, there is a recurring temptation to start using the sources of credit which is again available.

I succumbed to the temptation of consolidating debts many times in my pre-management days. Each time my financial stability declined. In addition to continuing the use of credit cards, repayment of consolidated debts were extended for a much longer period of time. Naturally, a longer repayment period increases the amount of interest paid on the borrowed money. There is little hope for a brighter financial future for most people as long as consumer credit is habitually used.

The safest way to get out of debt is "by the numbers." List each creditor, the monthly payment, and total amount owed to each. Use the following example as a guide.

DEBT ACCOUNTS PAYABLE[1]		
List All Debts Separately		
Accounts Owed	Total Due	Monthly Payments
1. Department store A	$ 600.00	$ 40.00
2. Department store B	700.00	35.00
3. Credit card A	300.00	15.00
4. Credit card B	1,200.00	60.00
5. Bank loan	1,800.00	110.00
TOTALS	$ 4,600.00	$ 260.00

Here's the strategy to reduce or eliminate your consumer debt. Stop using your credit cards, except for reimbursed business expenses. When credit cards are used for business, keep reimbursed funds separate from personal funds. To discontinue the use of credit cards will likely take some not-before-practiced discipline. However, we seldom can live with abandon without paying a penalty at some future date. Money mismanagement using consumer credit will require some sacrifice to reverse. Switching from credit to cash is among the first challenges when pursuing greater financial strength.

Next, focus on paying off the creditor with the smallest total balance. In the example, the smallest balance is owed to "credit card A." The interest rate on each debt is of little consequence. The objective is to free additional money as quickly as possible and to win a victory over money mismanagement. Monthly payments must continue to be paid on all debts, but commit any extra money received to paying off the creditor with the lowest balance.

When the first debt is paid in full, add the monthly

payment which is freed to the monthly payment of the next debt with the smallest total balance. In the example, the "department store A" has the next smallest balance. Add the $15 monthly payment freed from "credit card A" to the $40 monthly payment for "department store A." Now $55 monthly goes to department store A.

The first money management victory has been achieved, and debt repayment then will begin to accelerate. As each creditor is paid in full, climbing out of debt speeds up. It's an ecstatic feeling! You want to shout, "Free at last!" When all consumer debt is paid off, celebrate—then use cash!

• **Begin savings/emergency fund.**—When Sarah and I committed ourselves to money management, we had no money saved for emergencies, much less anything else. Some people may be stimulated by dangerous living, but not having an emergency fund is like playing Russian roulette with credit ratings, financial stability, and personal and family well-being.

One of the pleasant surprises of money management is how less often we have money emergencies. In premanagement days, a dead battery on the car or a sick child triggered what seemed like a horrendous money emergency. These emergencies still occur, but we expect them and allocate money for them beforehand. As in most planning and preparation for future events, the crises can often be defused before they happen.

How much emergency money should be accumulated, and where should it be kept? For most people, three months of spendable income is sufficient. However, if you're employed where contract negotiations typically cause you to be without income for more than three months, adjust your emergency funds accordingly. The same concern would also apply to self-employed persons.

Emergency money needs to be invested in plans which do not make it inaccessible for long periods of time. However, there usually are investment options available to receive a better interest rate than a pass-book savings account pays and still have the money readily available. A credit union, if you have access to one, would be one place to check. Most banks offer money-market accounts which permit writing a limited number of checks each month. Short-term certificates of deposit may be another option for a better interest rate. You will need to explore all of your options. The objective is to earn the best interest possible on your emergency money while keeping it accessible.

● **Plan for children's college.**—When we designed our first financial plan, we had made no specific provisions for our children's college education. Our oldest daughter was already in college, and our son and youngest daughter were in high school, a senior and a sophomore, respectively. We had simply included college costs in our other money-juggling acts. The extra expenses were the main reasons my wife had gone to work outside of the home.

However, we did have a general agreement with our children about their college expenses. They were responsible for earning their own spending money and money for their books. They were faithful either to work part-time during school terms or summers and breaks to earn their share for college expenses. We as parents were responsible for tuition and about one trip home for each per month.

With no money saved and no adequate plans for tuition, our children relied on grants and student loans. As our new financial plan progressed, we were able to commit more and more each year to college expenses, thus reducing the amount of student loans necessary. When the last child graduated, we continued our financial commitment to college expenses until all of the student loans we had agreed to pay for were settled. Three years after our youngest child graduated, repayment of the loans was completed.

Five-Year Goals

With a sense of wonder I reflect back on our first goals and our first experiences with our first intentional money-management plan. That warm November afternoon Sarah and I gathered our records together at the dining-room table had a sense of destiny about it. What we decided there turned out to be a life-changing, life-shaping experience. We sat down that afternoon filled with desperation. After two or three hours, hope replaced melancholy.

What happened during those hours? At the end of the day, we had no more money than when we had begun our planning. What we had was direction, and the goals we included in our five-year plans speedily contributed to our enthusiasm.

It will be obvious as you develop your goals that longer-range goals often require only repeating a one-year goal year-after-year. Putting yourself into a position to pay cash for automobiles is one example.

● **Pay cash for automobiles.**—Within five years and for the rest of our lives, we agreed, we would pay cash for our automobiles. To many consumers, that sounds totally insane. Frankly, at the time, I had no idea how we were going to follow through on this goal. We had two cars with over 80,000 miles on each of them, and we were mired in debt—but I had learned from my recent money-management studies that credit should not be used to purchase any item which depreciates in value. If the experts affirmed this was correct, I resolved to follow their advice.

Problems with cars had plagued me like a curse over the years. When Adam and Eve sinned, God cast them out of the Garden of Eden with this promise:

"Because of what you have done, the ground will be under a curse. You will have to work hard all your life to make it produce enough food for you. It will produce weeds and thorns, and you will have to eat wild plants. You will have to work hard and sweat to make the soil produce anything" (Gen. 3:17-19, TEV).

So, I developed a "theology of cars" that goes about like this: After so many people left the farm, and weeds and thorns were no longer obstacles to them anymore, God substituted car problems for weeds and thorns!

After more than a year into our money-management plan, our cars were still performing well. That was fantastic because our money growth had not yet reached a level which would have allowed for us to designate automobile-replacement funds. Then the accident happened. One of our cars was totaled. Money management and paying cash for all depreciating items purchased suddenly became more challenging!

We thought of three possible solutions. Our first decision was to invest the $1,500 insurance money we received for the wrecked car and make it with only one car for the family. You guessed it: after two weeks of this arrangement, we decided it was unworkable. I was riding the bus to work, but with so many drivers vying for the car I seldom saw it, much less had a chance to drive it.

We then considered the other two possible solutions. We could finance a replacement car. After all, we had made a commitment to pay cash for automobiles within five years, not eighteen months. By this time, though, our "pay-as-you-go" financial plan was working so well, it seemed like treason to finance a car. So we settled on the third option. The emergency money we had saved was not for automobile replacement, but we decided to use it, along with the insurance money, to buy the best car possible.

We paid cash for our first car! I found a government-lease car with less than 30,000 miles on it, which I bought for $2,400. It served us well for over three years. Since making our commitment to wiser money management, we have paid cash for nine automobiles. After the first one, here's how we did it—and how *you* can do it.

By anticipating when we will next replace each of our cars, the amount of money required is prorated monthly and deposited into an auto-replacement fund. We operate on a two-year replacement plan. Also, if we drive one of our cars on business and are reimbursed for mileage, the mileage money, less gasoline expenses, is deposited in the auto-replacement fund. If only an honorarium is received, we charge ourselves the cents-per-mile allowed by the IRS less cost of gasoline. On a two-year cycle enough money is available to replace our cars if necessary. If a car is performing well, we drive it beyond two years until replacement is needed.

To initiate your cash auto-replacement plan, follow these steps. When you would normally trade cars and use financing, drive your present car for at least another year. During that year, make monthly car payments to yourself. If you can afford to make the payments to someone else, then you can afford to pay yourself for driving your old car.

At the end of one year, use the money you have saved, plus the trade-in value of your old car, and pay cash for the best car possible within the limits of your buying power.

• You will save money by not paying interest. That money can then be used to stimulate faster growth of your money.

• You will often find a better car for your money because of more careful shopping.

• You will boost confidence in your money- management ability and exult in the joy of increased financial freedom.

After paying cash for your first car, continue the process until you have obtained the quality of car best suited for your needs.

The illustration which follows assumes a beginning car value of $2,000, a $275-per-month payment into a personal auto-replacement account, and a 10-percent-per-year depreciation on used cars purchased.

	PAYING CASH FOR AUTOMOBILES and trading each year					
Year	**Auto** **Value**		**Money** **Saved**		**Cash Value** **Available**	
1	$1,800	+	$3,300	=	$5,100	
2	4,500	+	3,300	=	7,800	
3	7,000	+	3,300	=	10,300	

To illustrate the wisdom of paying cash for cars as opposed to financing, assume that after three years the $10,300 car is new rather than used. Your increased net value the first time you switch from financing to paying cash for a new car of this value would be about $5,600.

IF NEW AUTO IS FINANCED

$10,300   car, less $2,000 trade-in = $8,300 financed
  8,300   financed at 12% X 3 years = $1,624 interest
  8,300   + $1,624 = $9,924 payback ($275 per month)

Three-year Comparison, Financing versus Cash

Using credit	=	$11,924	($2,000 + $1,624)
Paying cash	=	11,900	investment ($2,000 + $9,900)
Difference	=	24	less investment using cash

(However, after three years you would own a new car rather than a three-year-old car. The new car's value would be equivalent to three years' depreciation.) Thus:

Difference	=	$ 24	less investment with cash
		5,150	depreciation value
		435	interest earned on savings
Paying cash	=	$ 5,609	increased value in 3 years

The amount of increased value in three years is the result of switching from financing to cash for a new auto the first time. In subsequent years and trades, increased value will be only interest saved and interest earned.

Begin investments.—As I indicated under our first-year goals, we started an emergency fund immediately. (An emergency fund should not be considered an investment in the technical sense, though they do earn interest.) Money invested is money that you can live without if, because of an economic downturn or failure of an institution, you lose your money. That's why investments should not normally be pursued until a person or family has an adequate emergency fund and life insurance, with all other necessary expense items funded monthly.

In the fifth year of our management plan Individual Retirement Accounts were funded in full for both Sarah and me. After three years or so, these IRA funds were moved from certificates of deposit to self-directed mutual funds.

For most people, after buying a house, their next investment probably should be to fund a retirement program. When a person has 30 or more years until retirement, as little as $100 per month will fund a sizeable retirement benefit if invested aggressively. Many have found that some mutual funds provide beneficial diversification and aggressiveness, sometimes yielding an average of 15 percent annually. For example:

■ $100 @ 15% for thirty years = $ 692,327.96

■ $125 @ 15% for thirty years = $ 865,409.95
■ $150 @ 15% for thirty years = $1,038,491.94

Compare the difference if $100 per month is invested starting just five years earlier, for a total of 35 years:

■ $100 @ 15% for 35 years= $1,467,718.02

Only $6,000 more invested on the front end yields an additional $775,390.06 at the end of 35 years. A small amount of money invested for a long time can produce remarkable results.

Long-range Goals—Up to Twenty Years or More

Goals that reach out to 20 years or more at first may not be defined too well, but don't let lack of clarity keep you from at least stating long-range goals. Even extremely vague goals can often give unexpected direction.

Prepay house mortgage.—When we set our goals, what grabbed our attention was a mortgage which extended five years beyond my normal retirement at age 65. So our first long-range goal reached out 24 years to pay off the mortgage by the time I retired. We took no specific action on this goal for about six years.

Money was allocated for IRAs in the fifth year of our management plan. With this funding in place, in the sixth year we had additional funds to invest. That's when our long-range, mortgage-prepayment goal became operative. After five years, all other major goals had been accomplished or were in progress. The house goal was the next logical one to pursue.

My thoughts developed like this: Our goal is to eliminate the house mortgage by the time of my retirement.

We live in a house which, though adequate now, will be 45 years old at my retirement. The age of the house and other factors suggested many changes and repairs on the house up to and into retirement. We have always wanted to build a house, so why not invest in land and build a house for our retirement years?

With these possibilities guiding us, we began a search for unimproved property. After about six months of casual searching, we found property that was nearly ideal for our goal—in the location we desired and below market price. (It wasn't even up for sale. We simply went looking and asking. When shopping, patience is a virtue to cultivate.) In slightly over two years we had the property paid for. Within another year plans were drawn and construction started.

We were nine years into our management plan when building began. In those nine years we had increased our net worth significantly—to a level where one bank agreed to make a construction loan with me serving as general contractor. (Banks are reluctant to loan construction money when an experienced contractor is not used.) Serving as general contractor and doing some of the construction work ourselves, we increased our net worth almost $50,000 dollars in the process of building. Our goal of having a mortgage-free house moved up eight or nine years.

Our satisfying building experience caused us to set another goal. We plan to build again before retirement, probably soon. After our present house is sold and the construction costs paid, we will have the mortgage-free house we planned to have. Money management is fun, even if it sometimes involves hard, dirty work.

Continue investments for retirement.—With ongoing needs and retirement plans in place and funded, this last goal simply involves maintenance. To keep pace with inflation, funds accumulated will need to be managed for best returns and for safety. In retirement, given adequate health, we plan to be involved in long-term, foreign mission projects. If we have no major catastrophes between now and then, our only decisions will be where to go and how long to stay. Money needed should not be an issue.

What About You?

What are your goals? I consider my family more or less typical with goals similar to many other families. If we can successfully reach our goals, you can reach your goals too. You can adapt our goals to your needs, but your success depends on you. You must want to succeed and commit the mental and physical energy necessary to achieve those goals.

Hindrances That Can Rob Your Future

Why do so many people and families not have written, clearly defined goals to keep their energies focused? That's a prime question. Let's explore it.

Self-imposed Poverty

Some people are hindered by a desire for more things, usually insignificant baubles or trinkets, which make them poor. John Murray was like that. He typically had little cash in his wallet, sometimes not enough to buy a beggar a bowl of soup. John was barely keeping bank and credit card payments current, yet he couldn't resist the latest gadget that came on the market.

When the credit limit on one of his cards was paid down enough to permit another purchase, out he would go to snap up another gadget he had been coveting.

John was both rich and poor. He could act rich and feel rich when his credit-card balance would permit it. Most of the time, though, he felt dirt poor because his only goal was to make it until the next payday and the time when his credit card balance would allow for an additional purchase. He lived on dreams of what he might acquire next.

Sadly, John's mind-set and actions are probably typical for 50 percent or more of the U.S. population. The result is that many people feel like poor people most of the time, and poor people generally do not plan well for the future. Immediate needs dominate their thinking. How will I buy food and clothes? How will I pay the rent or mortgage next month?

It doesn't matter that John and most of the people in his situation have a median income or better. He's always broke, and he thinks poor. His primary goal is to make it until he's paid again. Any other goals are more like fantasies. "Maybe someday something miraculous will happen to change my financial situation for the better," he muses. "Maybe I'll inherit a lot of money. Maybe I'll find a bag of money that has fallen out of an armored truck. Maybe I'll win one of the sweepstakes I've entered."

Rationalization Is an Educated Excuse

Less-educated people may make excuses for inaction or for their less-than-best action. The more educated "rationalize." No matter the terminology, either one is usually empty justification. Rationalization more often justifies inferior actions which manage to prevent better actions. For example, a family finances a new car. The monthly payments on the car raise their debt payments to almost the maximum limit. With no discretionary funds, the family soon discovers that such goals as starting an emergency fund or paying cash for future automobiles become unrealistic.

The process that stops the goal-setting, however, starts with rationalizations which follow this general line: It's going to cost a lot to keep the old car repaired. Repairing the old car will be like throwing money down a hole. A new car will use less gasoline. Savings on repairs and gasoline mean that our payments on the new car won't be that much more than repairing and buying gasoline for the old car. Besides, we can't afford to be without a good car. Our parents live out of town, and they expect us to visit them regularly.

Rationalizations must be exposed for what they are, justifications to do what the emotions of an undisciplined life-style really want to do. Normally, it doesn't require a lot of money to maintain a well-kept older car. There are exceptions, but not many.

How much more will it really cost for gasoline for the old car than for the new one. Here's an example. Suppose a family drives a car 20,000 miles per year. A new car may get eight miles per gallon more than the old car, which is probably a generous assumption. Trading for a new car that increases miles-per-gallon by eight miles will save about $6 per week or $312 per year. That's about one month's car payment—certainly not justification for postponing significant life-changing goals in order to have a new car.

When it's necessary to keep an older car in order to accomplish more meaningful life goals, consider renting a car for longer, out-of-town trips. On trips of short duration but of several miles, it's usually more economical to rent a car than drive the family car. For your next trip, compare what rental car charges and gasoline would cost in comparison with the cost of driving your own car based on a cost of about 30 cents per mile. (The Internal Revenue Service reimbursement cost per mile is currently just under 30 cents per mile, but the American Automobile Association's estimated cost per mile for owning and operating a mid-size car is over 30 cents.)

Ignorance Can Be Dangerous

Some people may have set no financial goals because of ignorance—not because they are mentally retarded or lack natural, intellectual ability, but sometimes because they were never told that goal-setting was important. Like other cultural traditions that keep parents from instructing their children in certain matters, the importance of goals is often ignored. About the only encouragement to set goals I received from my dad was, "Go to school and save all of the money you can save."

"Get all of the education you can," he would advise. "I don't want you to be like me." Most of Dad's counsel was on target, and I more or less followed through on the advice to get an education. I was aware that education could help one make more money—but education generally doesn't teach you how to set life goals and manage the money you make to reach those goals. Some college-educated people don't even know how to balance their checkbooks, much less make wise management decisions. These people are functionally illiterate in financial matters.

It seems that culture, which keeps parents from teaching their children about such goals, also influences education. Both the family and the educational system seem to assume that we will intuitively know how to set goals and organize our lives around them. *The focus of education is on how to earn money, not achieve a full and meaningful life with the money we earn.* Ignorance can be dangerous to your future. It's our responsibility to educate ourselves about managing money with wisdom.

Notes

1. Anthony Robbins, *Unlimited Power* (New York: Fawcett Columbine Books, cited in *Communication Briefings,* December 1987), 3.

2. Adapted from *Christian Money Management Workbook* published by the SBC Stewardship Commission, Nashville, TN, 5.

Size Up Your Financial Strength

A husband and father of three preteen children was being interviewed by an international corporation. The possibility of world travel and a lucrative contract appealed to the young executive.

The interviewer sensed the man had some fine qualities that would be an asset to the corporation. However, being a father himself and knowing the pressure such a job would place on the young family, he felt responsible. So he decided to used a hypothetical situation to determine the prospective employee's maturity and values.

"If I offered you a ten-year, $2 million contract ($200 thousand per year), could you accept it? Keep in mind that extensive, extended travel will be necessary."

"I certainly could," the prospect answered quickly, thinking how much better the contract was than he had anticipated.

Continuing, the interviewer asked, "What if I could offer you only $500 thousand, $50 thousand per year plus expenses? Would you accept the job?"

Disappointed but wanting to appear decisive and firm the young man answered, "No, I could not! You would have to pay me more than $50 thousand to be away from home most of the time. What kind of husband and father do you think I am?"

"I believe we've established that," the interviewer noted with some remorse. "All we're doing now is negotiating a price."[1]

Eagerness to be successful financially sometimes distorts value judgments. Often more money is not what a person or family needs to accomplish goals, but wise management to inspire work and enhance the use of income received.

You see, income can be viewed as a status symbol or growth potential. Often, when status is important to a person, income is used ineffectively. Impressing other people with position, money, and possessions and getting maximum benefit from income tend to be mutually exclusive. When honorable goals and priorities are not followed intentionally, the result is a life-style shaped by the fallout of people's excesses. Ideally, spendable income as determined from the activity in this chapter will be managed to achieve the goals chosen in the previous chapter.

To help relate your goals to your income, consider these objectives. In broad strokes they represent what your income can wisely be used for.

Objectives

Goals differ from one person to another and from one family to another. Therefore, people use their income differently. Current age, age of children, or special circumstances—such as a family member needing special care—will influence goal-setting and the use of income. But there are some objectives which are common to most people.

Providing for Oneself and/or One's Family[2]

This objective is universal. Yet, often there are one or two matters that complicate this objective. When setting goals to guide your money management, determine if there are unusual factors which make providing for yourself or your family particularly difficult. A chronic illness or more-than-usual, job-related automobile expenses are examples.

When there is an area of special need, concentrate on solving it by making it a primary goal. For example, maybe one of your children has a chronic illness. Rather than letting this source of financial strain rob you of any hope for making your money grow, attack it head-on. Rise to the challenge! As a primary goal, when you allocate income to expenses, make provisions for the special need and then adjust other life-style and spending decisions to accommodate the primary goal. Treat the money necessary for the special need as a fixed expense and then focus on maximizing what income is left. In certain cases it may be advisable to look for opportunities to increase income, at least temporarily.

Being a Good Citizen[3]

Using resources for citizenship includes paying necessary taxes and making charitable contributions. The percentage of your income required for taxes is somewhat flexible, but not as flexible as other areas of spending. We should pay all of the taxes we owe, but not more than we need to pay. Wise money management includes learning about legal tax deductions which can save you from 15 to more than 30 percent of your income used to pay taxes.

Giving to charity is another way to be a good citizen. No other place in the world benefits more from charitable contributions than the people of North America. Contributions to non-profit organizations help millions of people each year and usually provide tax deductions.

Using a portion of income for citizenship is responsible money management. The more you make your money grow, the more helpful you can be to people who need your help. Good management can even reduce or eliminate resentfulness about paying taxes.

Doing Works of Faith[4]

People of faith recognize that conscientious money management can help them accomplish yet another objective. God created people to represent Him in the world.[5] Every person, Christian or not, is a manager of the material gifts which God provides.[6] Each person is also accountable for the use of these provisions. Christians represent God by using a percentage of their income to help other people. Gifts given to your church help share the gospel in the community where your church is located. In many churches, a percentage of members' gifts is used to send the gospel to other parts of the world.

The Greek word translated *steward* means "a manager of something which belongs to someone else." Everything belongs to God,[7] and we are His managers. As

God's managers, we disburse (dispense, distribute) the resources He provides for us, which is described by the verb form of the Greek word for steward.[8] Our English word *economics* comes from the same Greek word as steward. Also, the English word *steward* is derived from two Anglo-Saxon words, *stig* and *weird,* which mean "keeper of a pigpen"! That is, managing something that belongs to someone else.

For Christians, giving to our churches to communicate the gospel and help people in need is an integral part of our management responsibility. When we give to God through our churches we worship Him, confess our faith in Christ, and serve other people in His name.

Benefits from Estimating Income

Knowing spendable income is essential for developing a workable budget. Obviously, if you try to budget and spend gross income, when taxes become due you'll be in trouble. Also, completing the income form may help you discover incidental income which can be used for faster growth of your money.

However, there is another benefit which may be as important to your well-being as the more evident ones. I'm intentionally encouraging you to compute your gross income to see any fringe benefits provided for you. Many people have health, accident, and/or life insurance provided by their company. Others have additional benefits such as a retirement annuity or profit sharing. If you have any or all of these benefits, be grateful. Such benefits are a part of the provisions a gracious God has made for you. "Otherwise, you may say in your heart, 'My power and the strength of my hand made me this wealth.' But you shall remember the Lord your God, for it is He who is giving you power to make wealth."[9]

Step 2: Estimate Your Income
Completing the Income Form

Think about your income. It provides necessities for your livelihood and the potential for reaching your goals. Hopefully, in families where both spouses work, all income will be considered equal. Viewing and treating multiple incomes as his and hers reduces the possibility of effective management and the likelihood of accomplishing significant goals.

INCOME FORM	
Salary(s)	$ 32,144.00
Self-employment Income	0
Interest Income	825.00
Social Security Income	0
Pension Income	0
Other Income (Hobby)	1,000.00
Total Annual Income	$ 33,969.00
Less Income Taxes	$ 2,700.00
Less Social Security Taxes	4,243.00
Less Other Deductions ( )	0
Annual Spendable Income	$ 27,026.00
(Divided by 12 equals)	
Monthly Spendable Income	$ 2,252.16

Also, any workable management plan must be based on reality, not ballpark figures. Therefore, to be accurate you may need to locate recent payroll check stubs and other sources of income information. Work with the income you have now and will have until the next change in income occurs. As you complete the income form, read the discussion which follows for instructions. The results will be used later in Step 4 when you begin to develop your budget.

The objective of the income form is to arrive at monthly spendable income. The salary(s) line includes income as an employee(s) from which an employer(s) withholds income and Social Security taxes. However, to get a big picture of your income, record gross (before-tax) income on the first line.

Self-employment income is income on which you're responsible for paying income taxes and Social Security taxes, usually quarterly. It could be from a full-time or a part-time business. To determine spendable income from a business, all expenses for operating the business and taxes are deducted. However, when a self-employed person develops a budget in Step 4, the taxes must be included as income and made a part of one's budget. Expenditures for taxes must be paid as other expenses, either monthly or quarterly. (This applies to ordained ministers also, even though churches are required to provide ministers with a W-2 form instead of a 1099.)

Line three, interest income, also includes income from dividends. It is included on the income form only if you actually receive and use it for living expenses or for another type of investment. If interest and dividend income is automatically reinvested, be grateful for it, but omit such income when determining spendable income. However, interest and dividend income not used for living expenses would be reflected in your net worth statement.

Social Security and pension income pertains mostly to retired persons. The other income line may include a money-producing hobby, child support, alimony, etc. The important thing when recording income from whatever source is to determine how much money you have to use to accomplish your goals. Unless you identify all sources of income and use all income effectively, it can vanish without accomplishing anything tangible.

Here's an example of incidental income and what it can be worth. For a time I did some moonlighting which produced about $50 per month income. As self-employed income, I received a 1099 form each year indicating my earnings. Before I committed to a money-management plan, I deposited the $50 into my checking account, and it disappeared. Because I didn't use the money for a beneficial purpose, at year-end when I had to pay income tax and Social Security on it, the extra income became a liability rather than an advantage.

Suppose, however, I had invested this $50 per month in a good no-load mutual fund. Before taxes, $50 invested per month earning 12 percent interest will yield $24,979 in just 15 years. (Twelve percent is a good interest rate; however, 15 percent is often possible.) By letting money work for you, in 15 years $50 per month can grow to $139 per month with little additional expenditure of energy. At 15 percent earned interest, the same investment becomes $33,425 or $186 per month.

If you start younger and have 30 years to invest $50 per month at 15 percent, the end results will be $346,164. Amazing! You earn $50 each month, and your money earns another $911 per month.

On the income form, when all income has been reduced by taxes and other deductions such as health insurance, you will have determined your annual spendable income. Divide the annual figure by 12 for your monthly spendable income. Since most expenditures are monthly, the suggested budget in Step 4 will be a monthly budget, which is the reason to determine your monthly spendable income.

What's Inside a Disclaimer

Now that you have an accurate income figure, how do you feel about the amount of your income? Whether you're feeling smug or a bit depressed, I encourage you not to start thinking up disclaimers to excuse further work toward a good management plan.

If your income is a comfortable amount, you may be tempted to respond as do some people I meet in my conferences. They make sure I know before the conference starts that they're not there because of money problems. Their disclaimer often goes something like this: "I didn't need to come to this meeting. I'm not having any trouble paying my bills, and I have a little money left over each month. I just came because a friend asked me to come."

I usually respond with questions. Have you written out your financial goals for the next twenty years or more? Do you have an adequate emergency fund? Are you paying cash for your automobiles? Do you pay charge card purchases in full each month? Is your house paid for? Will your retirement income be sufficient in the year you retire? Are you earning at least 12 percent on your investments? More often than not, they answer "no" to most of these questions. Then I suggest that they can benefit from a study on money management. "If you're paying all of your bills with some money left over each month, think what you can do if you manage your money for maximum growth."

I meet more people, however, who try to justify muddling though life with no management plans because of a perceived lack of income. Their disclaimer is, "I don't make enough money to manage." Logically, the smaller one's income, the better that person needs to manage his or her money. So why do many people with average or less than average incomes think they don't make enough money to manage?

Familiarity

We often become comfortable with the way we do things. Even if we suspect or someone suggests there is a better way, we resist because change means we must learn something new. If we're really under pressure financially, we may feel we can't cope with yet another change. "At-home" feelings often keep people stuck in a rut. When we allow ourselves to stay chained to a familiar, unproductive routine, there's no hope for financial growth. Observe people who are stuck in the welfare system.

Fear

Sometimes, we reason, it's best just not to know our economic status. We think if we look at all of the facts we may discover we really are financially sick. Also, many people fear money management because it seems so difficult to understand, maybe even a bit mysterious. Fear can paralyze productive decisions and actions.

Loss of Freedom

As did my wife, who for years resisted a budget, many people think money management (a budget) will limit their freedom. But a closer look may reveal the real culprit. The argument for loss of freedom may be a disguise for fear or lack of understanding. Because, in reality, good money management increases freedom. Sarah is quick to verify this fact. She affirms that she has more freedom now with money than ever before. Certainly the choices of where to spend have increased, as well as having more money to spend.

Whatever the basis for a disclaimer, the result is often an inability to make wise decisions about money. But let me illustrate what can be done through wise money management, even on a small income.

A young minister's wife, Joan Milleson, attended a promotion conference on money management. I illustrated the five steps and the possible outcome of a working money management plan. Joan made no response during the meeting, but afterwards stopped by to visit with me.

She said, "I'm so happy I chose this conference tonight. Now I better understand and appreciate what my husband has been doing. He has done all of the things you have suggested since we married eight years ago. We don't make much money and never have, but we pay cash for everything except the house we bought. At times I've resented him for refusing to charge anything, especially when I wanted more clothes for the children, but now I'm grateful for what he's doing. I'll encourage him more in the future."

Rather than being paralyzed by a low income, Allen Milleson was energized and took positive actions. In my discussion with Joan, I discovered that their income was only 60 to 70 percent of the average income of other families in the area. In fact, with two children they might have been close to qualifying for food stamps. Yet they owned a dependable car, for which they paid cash, and were able to qualify for a mortgage on a small house. Good money management has its rewards; excuses don't.

Increase Income or Cut Expenses?

More people than not have financial problems. Realistically, they either need to increase income or cut expenses. But is more income always beneficial? When squeezed financially, people look for solutions. Not wanting to reduce their standard of living, the most appealing resolution is to increase income rather than to reduce expenses. For families, the most frequent action is for the wife to seek employment outside of the home, if not already employed. The assumption is that any increase in income will be helpful. Is this a valid assumption?

Not always. A family should evaluate the real value

of a second income rather than assuming it will be helpful. Increased income less the extra cost of earning it will reveal the net increase in buying power. At the time my family embarked on our new money-management plan, I was surprised when I subjected my wife's income to careful analysis. I discovered that it was costing as much or more for her to work outside of the home as she was earning.

Sarah worked 32 hours per week as a receptionist in the late 1970's. Her annual salary was $7,800. Using our records and input she gave about spending habits, a compilation was made. Here's the breakdown of her work expenses.

COST FOR SPOUSE'S EMPLOYMENT

$ 546	Income tax withholdings
492	Social Security taxes
51	Other withholdings
720	Transportation
936	Church gifts (Weekly and mission)
520	Extra clothes, cleaning, etc.
2,400	Additional cost for food and household operation
780	"I deserve it because I'm working" and gifts at the office
1,374	Additional taxes due to higher income tax bracket
$ 7,819	Total cost to be employed

These calculations were made after we started our management plan and after Sarah had quit work. Therefore, we may have been able to more realistically and accurately determine some of the expenses. For example, the "additional cost for food and household operation" is a reliable figure. The savings resulted from more careful meal-planning and buying less junk food. When Sarah had outside employment, we stopped almost daily to buy something at the grocery store. Those frequent stops caused us to buy soft drinks, chips, etc., more frequently. More careful meal planning made eating less expensive and reduced the number of trips to the grocery store. Fewer shopping trips eliminated much of the junk food we were buying.

If you do similar calculations for your family, yours will likely be different. For example, we did not have one of the big-ticket items which many families incur when the wife takes outside employment. We didn't have child care expenses. Another possible expense item is parking or longer commuting distances.

The analysis of Sarah's employment is based solely on the economic benefits of her working outside of the home. There could be other determining factors. A wife may choose to work based on career goals, her contribution to society, or personal fulfillment without consideration for family economics. Also, adverse family circumstances have forced many wives to seek employment. Some choose to work temporarily to help their husband or children achieve career goals including adequate education. These are value decisions each family must make for themselves.

As a rule of thumb, increased income will not improve a person's finances if no other positive management actions are taken. Expenses simply increase to match income or worse. Often, when income is increased, people qualify for and incur more debt. The end result is a worsened financial condition. There is no substitute for wise money management.

How Income Can Be Profitably Increased

The illustration above is not to suggest that you should never attempt to increase income. Most of the ideas and principles I've presented in this book will help increase your income, first by increasing your buying and investing power. Also, I believe in hard work and developing skills to their utmost. The ideal is to reach a balance between maximum income production and family, Christian, and community duties.

One way to increase income potential is to master a specific skill. *Specializing* is the word I use to describe this concept of skill development. *Specializing* means "to become better than average" or "an authority" in some subject or area of work. This idea can be used in the context of your present employment or as an avocation.

I don't recall when the idea of specializing became a part of my philosophy, but I've practiced it most of my life. I used it in high school basketball, during my tenure in the Air Force, when I worked for the United States Postal Service, and when a minister.

Specializing is how I got into stewardship development. I planned after graduate school to become proficient in some area of ministry. I knew our denomination used people with special interests and skills to help lead conferences. Circumstances and need caused me to become involved in stewardship development. My involvement in stewardship led to more graduate study. As planned, I became a state convention special worker. In four years my avocation became my primary ministry.

After moving to a full-time stewardship position with the national convention, I specialized again. One area of my stewardship work was money management. Because of my own need and interest, I begin to research, write, and lead conferences on the subject. As in the past, my specializing has been most satisfying personally and has also provided a way to help other people. Maybe you have a hobby or interest you can develop. Bud Winthrope had a good, dependable job he enjoyed, but he was fascinated with automobiles. His thrill was buying cars and trucks in basically good mechanical condition and restoring them, usually with cleanup and minor repairs. At first, Bud used his hobby to provide low-cost transportation for himself and his wife. Then gradually his hobby began to produce income. He buys a car or truck and uses it for his own transportation while he restores it. After restoration is complete, he continues to drive it while offering the automobile for sale and looking for another one to restore.

Sometimes, Bud has two automobiles and occasionally none. (His wife does become a bit frustrated when she has to provide him with transportation, but it's usually only for a few days at a time.) His objective is to keep his investment as low as possible.

Note what Bud's hobby is providing. He has inexpensive transportation, a lot of enjoyment, and significant incidental income. He's using most of the income from three to five auto sales each year to supplement his retirement plan at work. And he's looking forward to retirement when his hobby can become a second vocation.

Do you have an interest or hobby that has the potential to produce income? It should be a pursuit for which you have a genuine concern and/or curiosity. If an interest or hobby can produce income, that's great. However, there are benefits other than income which extra curricular activities provide. And it's not necessary that they produce income to provide other benefits—fulfillment, enjoyment, relaxation, self-worth, and/or a beneficial contribution to the lives of people. If you embark on an enterprise just for the money, it likely will become laborious and will defeat the objective an interest or hobby should provide.

Another possibility for increasing income or self-worth is to upgrade your skills by going back to school. An advanced degree in your present profession or a degree in your area of interest may provide more income. Even if it doesn't yield more income immediately, increased self-confidence and skills often result in promotions and higher-income levels.

Many years ago a wise and faithful man set forth a worthy work ethic. He wrote, "Let him who steals steal no longer; but rather let him labor, performing with his own hands what is good, in order that he may have something to share with him who has need."[10] Good work is the first objective, work which produces an income and is beneficial to society. Second, work is more rewarding when some of the income earned is used to help other people. Helping others enriches the person providing the help and the person or persons receiving it.

I can suggest how you can better manage your money and increase your buying power. I can illustrate how you can increase your income. But I can't change who you are—your life-style and commitments. Who you are and what you do with your money is mostly determined by your values. And I've observed that when a person's values are askew, usually much of the rest of that person's life is also tilted off center, including the use of money and other material things.

Earning adequate income and managing it wisely is up to you. Continue to read and learn.

What Is Your Net Worth?

Since you've established your income, and as you begin your pilgrimage in money management, it's a good time to calculate your net worth also. This exercise provides a similar benefit as determining your spendable income except on a cumulative basis.

You may be surprised to see the value of your estate, even if your money management has not been ideal to this point. Further, knowing your net worth as you commit to wiser management will provide a point of reference. Recalculating your net worth annually is one of several ways to gauge the growing benefits of prudent money management.

NET WORTH[11]	
Assets and Liabilities (Husband & Wife)	**Dollar Value**
ASSETS: (What you own)	
Cash on hand	$ 90.00
Checking account(s) balance	1,812.00
Savings account(s) balance	8,800.00
Credit Union savings	0
Bonds, stocks, securities	6,500.00
Cash value of life insurance	0
Cash value of retirement plans	33,210.00
Real estate (market value)	90,000.00
Automobiles (market value)	7,500.00
Furnishing, equipment, tools	5,500.00
Jewelry, collections, clothing	3,200.00
Money owed to us	0
Other assets (computer)	600.00
TOTAL ASSETS	**$ 157,212.00**
LIABILITIES: (What you owe)	
Home mortgage	$ 71,000.00
Other real estate	0
Home improvement loan	0
Loan on car	0
Bank loans (school loan)	2,300.00
Charge cards (bank, gasoline, etc.)	0
Medical bills	0
Other debts	0
TOTAL LIABILITIES	**$ 73,300.00**
To find net worth:	
TOTAL ASSETS	**$ 157,212.00**
Less TOTAL LIABILITIES	**$ 73,300.00**
NET WORTH	**$ 83,912.00**
Recalculate annually	

Notes

1. Adapted from an illustration by James G. Carr, "Selective Ethics," *Piedmont Airlines Magazine,* May 1986, 22.

2. First Timothy 5:8.

3.   Matthew 22:21; Romans 13:5-7.

4. Acts 2:44-45; 1 Corinthians 9:11-15; 2 Corinthians 8—9; Philippians 4:15-19.

5. Genesis 1:26.

6. Genesis 1:28

7. Psalm 24:1.

8. Luke 16:2: "You can no longer be my distributer."

9.   Deuteronomy 8:17-18 (NASB). Also, see Psalm 24:1ff.; Proverbs 10:22; Matthew 5:45; Hebrews 6:7.

10. Ephesians 4:28 (NASB).

11. Adapted from *Christian Money Management Workbook* (FS-1) published by the SBC Stewardship Commission, Nashville, TN, October 1991, 16.

Where Is Your Money Going?

"When the going gets tough, the tough go shopping." Do we joke about spending money to temper what we know to be the seriousness of it? Spending money can be a sobering task, but it can be an equally joyous experience. To some degree, each time we spend money we impact our future positively or negatively.

How Should We Appraise Money and Material Things?

Getting and using money is a significant part of our lives. Someone has estimated that we use as much as 80 percent of our waking hours making, spending, and thinking about money. Whether that's true or not, I do know that many people have a high regard for money. We should be aware, however, that people appraise money and material things differently. Even in the general population, there are several dissimilar views about money.

Money Is Bad

It may surprise you that some people think money and material things are bad. A religious philosophy called Gnosticism, which dates back to the first or second century (A.D.), taught that the universe was a prison and that the earth was a dungeon which imprisoned people. Release for Gnostics was to escape the influence of the evil world by gaining superior knowledge (from Greek, *gnosis*).[1] Holding this view made it impossible for them to embrace anything material and manage it well. Money and all material things were bad.

I suppose there have been people ever since who have held to the Gnostic view of money to some degree. In the 1960s, for example, a counter culture or alternate life-style developed in the United States which renounced wealth to some degree. Adherents wore ragged clothes, the men grew beards and long hair, the women dressed down their femininity, and some of them rejected single family housing for crowded communes. At least by their actions, they repudiated the money and wealth of society around them. A few of these people are still around.

Money Has No Value

We haven't had much contact with people of this mind-set in the past, but it's changing. As Eastern religions grow and become more active in the world, especially in the United States, people who hold this view of money and material things will become more prominent. Hindus and Buddhists in particular embrace this belief. "The Hindu refers to the material world as Maya, which means a 'temporary, worthless illusion.' The Buddhist, on the other hand, would not hold that the material is unreal, but neither would he ascribe value to it."[2] Both groups reach similar conclusions—

money and material things have no significance to people.

Money Has Ultimate Value

In the Western world we may be more familiar with the view that money and material things are "the" reality or have ultimate value. This is an exaggerated view of Jewish and Christian teachings which affirm that material things are inherently good.[3] If pressed, most of us would admit that people are more important than money, but then quickly confess that some people will do anything for money, even kill.

Money Is Valuable, Not of Ultimate Value

I believe there is a middle ground, and I believe a majority of the general population embraces this view. I'm also realistic enough to know that if a line is drawn representing the middle-ground view of money, very few people could actually stand on the line. Most of us may think we are standing on the line when, in fact, we're standing a little to one side or the other.

There also seems to be a discrepancy between what we say we value and what we practice. In his book, *What Americans Believe,* George Barna lists ten things people value.[4] Number one was *family* with 94 percent; last of the ten values was *money* with 33 percent. The other side of the coin is an extremely high divorce rate, over 50 percent—money is a major contributing factor in 70 percent or more of family conflicts. We may place greater value on family, but money and its use make up a leading problem.

How do you feel about money? Does spending money cause you and/or other family members problems? It's important to get in touch with your feelings about money, whichever side of the line you're standing on. To admit that you place a different value on money than your spouse or friends is a first step in resolving both inward and outward conflicts. A personal struggle with the value of money or struggles with a spouse can effectively thwart any attempt to manage your money better.

Acknowledge your present money value position and that of others and evaluate your current spending patterns without judgment. Admit that money can be used in ways which are detrimental to other people, but that in our thoroughly economic society it's a necessary commodity. It can also be used to enhance our lives and the lives of others. The knowledge gained from cataloging expenses may be exactly the information needed to resolve any existing conflicts. And it surely will provide the facts needed to build a workable budget in Step 4. Work with anticipation of success.

Step 3: Determine Your Expenses for Last Year

Discovering what you spend your money for will serve at least two purposes. First, an allocation cannot be made without some basis-in-fact. A workable budget must allocate money equitably to item categories. Second, knowing your expenses will help evaluate any out-of-balance spending. Without a budget, some items often demand and receive a disproportionate amount of our income. In effect, an analysis of spending may reveal life-style patterns which are thwarting some goal accomplishment heretofore thought unattainable. Success may be as simple and uncomplicated as a spending adjustment.

DETERMINE EXPENSES[5]	
Account Items	Monthly Average Expenses Last Year
1. Church gifts	$ 280.00
2. Home mortgage	580.00
3. Home insurance	
4. Home taxes	
5. Savings & emergency	60.00
6. Income taxes	
7. Social Security	
8. Retirement	
9. Life insurance	43.00
10. Health & accident ins.	
11. Hospital insurance	
12. Auto insurance	50.00
13. Loan payment	
14. Total other debts	75.00
15. Food	240.00
16. Clothing	75.00
17. Gas	
18. Electricity	90.00
19. Water	22.00
20. Telephone	35.00
21. Home improvements	
22. Home furnishings	32.00
23. Home maintenance	25.00
24. Auto repair	40.00
25. Auto gasoline & oil	70.00

26. Auto license	6.00
27. Medical & dental	40.00
28. Medications	20.00
29. Hospital	30.00
30. Subscriptions	3.00
31. School expenses	50.00
32. Cleaning, laundry	10.00
33. Allowances	20.00
34. Toiletries, cosmetics	10.00
35. Recreation, vacation	30.00
36. Gifts, birthday, weddings	20.00
37. Christmas	50.00
38. Other	5.16
Total	$ 2,001.16

Where Does the Money Go?

The objective of Step 3 is to determine your average monthly expenses for item categories. Unlike Step 2 when you looked forward to the next anticipated change in income, in this step you look back at your expenses for the past twelve months. The results will be a graph of your expenses.

Expenditures can be divided into two main categories—fixed expenses and flexible expenses. On the expense form above, items 1—14 reflect typical fixed expenses and items 15—38 are typical flexible expenses. As you complete the form, ignore those items which do not apply to you and add items unique to your expenses. Your checkbook register, receipts, documents, and bills should provide the information you will need to complete the expense form.

Fixed expenses.—There usually are two kinds of fixed expenses—those which must be paid monthly and those which are paid quarterly, semiannually, or annually. Fixed expenses such as the mortgage (rent) or loan payment which are paid monthly are easy to determine. Record the monthly amounts as they appear in your checkbook register or elsewhere.

Fixed expenses paid in three-, six-, or twelve-month installments take slightly more effort. For example, if "auto insurance" is paid in six-month intervals divide the amount due by six to ascertain the monthly amount. Record the monthly amount on the form. Follow this procedure until all fixed expenses, items 1—14, are completed.

As you work on fixed expenses, be aware that you may not need to record some expenses because they are withheld from your income or included with another payment. Employees who work for an employer should not record income taxes and Social Security in this step since these taxes are deducted from your income in Step 2. However, self-employed persons who pay taxes quarterly should include them in this step. Home insurance and property taxes usually are included with the mortgage payment. If so, omit these two items.

Item 13, "loan payment," is for a major payment other than the mortgage, maybe a car or a home improvement loan. Item 14, "total other debts," is for the combined total of revolving-charge purchases. This item is placed in fixed expenses particularly for those who want to eliminate their consumer debt. (See chapter 1 under Goals for Next Year.) Setting a fixed payment at or above the monthly minimum payment and maintaining it, even when the creditor reduces the minimum payment, will eliminate debt faster.

If charge cards are used after a budget is developed and implemented, items charged should be planned for in the appropriate item accounts. If a medical expense is charged on a bank card, it should be deducted from the medical expenses account. Therefore, the "total other debts" item would not be used, and the monthly payment amount can remain fixed.

Flexible Expenses.—As the name implies, expenses for items 15—38 on the form fluctuate from one month to the next. However, some of the expenses are easier to determine than others because of the records associated with them. Utility bills normally are received monthly and designed with two parts, one to keep and one to return with the payment. Even if the receipts are not kept, many people routinely use checks to pay utilities bills and have the checkbook register from which this information can be obtained. Also, utility companies usually will provide printouts of charges for the past year.

Ideally, the monthly average for each flexible expense item will be determined and recorded. Using receipts or your checkbook register, add up the amount paid for the past twelve months and then divide by twelve. The example for electricity which follows is an example of how the average for each item can be determined.

AVERAGING COST FOR ELECTRICITY			
January	$130	July	$ 90
February	140	August	100
March	100	September	80
April	80	October	60
May	60	November	70
June	70	December	100
		Annual Total:	$1,080

Monthly average: $1,080 ÷ 12 = $90

What do you do about expenses for which there are no complete records? You can use one of two options; you can "guesstimate" the average monthly cost for each item. The accuracy of this option will depend on your length of experience and involvement. After several years of paying for expenses, most of us have an impression of what things cost even if we don't keep records. However, a young person or couple just out of college will not have the advantage of experience to use this option.

I witnessed one young person who attempted to estimate expenses without real-life experiences to draw upon. It was a depressing moment to discover, when the monthly expenses were totaled, that income from the first "real" job after college was several hundred dollars short of the estimate needed.

The remaining option is a combination of using records and estimating, but within the limits of your income. Complete the items for which there are records and then estimate and distribute the balance of income to necessary expenses. This option helps maintain the ideal budget situation where expenses do not exceed income.

How Are You Doing?

After completing the expense form, your spending patterns should be evident. Is there some expense item that's out of proportion to your other expenses? Once in a conference at this point, one family's largest expenditure was miscellaneous. Obviously, they had not completed the form with much care. Any expense they couldn't identify was assigned to miscellaneous. What about your spending patterns?

Is There a Problem with Debt?

At this point in the process, Bill and Sherry Gallespi realized just how much they owed on credit cards from banks and department stores. They were stunned to discover that about 40 percent of their spendable income was needed to make monthly payments on their indebtedness. They admitted to having struggled to keep payments current, even getting cash advances on one bank card to make payments on others. Attributing their problem to being young and just getting started in life, they never dreamed their debt load was so out of proportion to their income.

Using credit cards is addictive.—Often when people acquire credit cards, it's for the noblest of reasons. They need a credit card for identification to cash checks. Or they obtain a card in case they have a medical or travel emergency. They promise themselves no charge purchases will be made except for emergencies. I

understand their reasoning and feelings. Given the economics of our society, I would not want to be without a
major credit card.

However, I have observed that the use of credit cards
can be addictive. And when some people try to banish
their cards, they have withdrawal symptoms. Here's an
example. Lloyd McSheer gave his college-bound son a
bank card. He reasoned that since his son would be 200
miles from home, a travel emergency was a likely possibility. In his father-son talk, Lloyd instructed his son
not to use the credit card except in an emergency.

All was well for several months. Then the son came
home one weekend and presented Lloyd with a charge
receipt and the money to pay for the charge. When
asked why the charge was made, the son said he was at
a concert, wanted a tape, but didn't have the money.
Lloyd explained again that the charge card was for
emergencies only.

A few months with no problems ended when the son
presented his dad with another charge receipt for gasoline and requested that the cost be deducted from expense money he would normally receive later. The
son's explanation was that he didn't have money for
gasoline to drive home. Lloyd explained to his son that
coming home was not an emergency; that he either
could have planned for the trip or postponed it. He cau-
tioned his son to use the card only for emergencies.
When an identical experience happened within a few
months, Lloyd promised to take back the charge card if
it was abused again.

Note how an addictive pattern begins to emerge. The
son used the charge card because he didn't have cash

with him—convenient use of the charge card. No harm seemed to have been done. The bill was paid in full even before necessary. With the second charge purchase, the son spent money before he received it—buy now, pay later. By the time the third charge purchase was made, but still below awareness, the son had been conditioned to relax his need to plan ahead for expenses.

The next step, for those who are not responsible to a dad like Lloyd's son, is to pay only the minimum payment on the monthly bill. By this point the addiction to credit has taken root. At first, minimum payments may be made to hold onto cash, rationalizing that a need for cash may present itself which is more urgent than paying off charge purchases. It's not long, however, until only the minimum payment can be made. Addiction to credit use becomes a way of life.

Over-indebtedness may reflect a compulsive behavior problem.—Debt may appear to be a serpent, slithering here and there seeking its prey. So it seemed to me, having experienced the ravages of its cunning deception myself, and now having dealt with the havoc it has caused in the lives of other people. However, debt proneness is not caused by an external force. And as with other debilitating, compulsive-behavior problems, some people need help to cope with overspending and excessive use of debt.

I mentioned earlier that we often joke about money. We also make light of debt. I've heard people jokingly say, "I've signed my life away" when buying a house or an automobile. I've heard men comment that they have "mortgaged everything except my wife." The truth is some have mortgaged their wives, too, at least their wives' earning power because both incomes have been used to obtain credit. Debt is no joking matter. People who overextend debt and people who are addicted to mind-altering substances have some common traits.

Comparing overspending and overextending debt to alcohol and drug addiction, psychotherapist Gloria Arenson writes that "the behaviors of spending and debting are not the real problem. The underlying problem is that most of us don't know how to solve the life problems arising from stressful situations and relationships. Compulsive urges to shop and to have 'things' are ways we distract ourselves from our real issues and our intense negative feelings."[6]

If overuse of debt and other compulsive behavior problems are internal and not caused by some outside "thing" which afflicts us, where is help to be found? Arenson says: "Living a life out-of-balance is not a disease. The behaviors we develop to try to feel good again are not the result of disease. They are 'syndromes,' a set of concurrent emotions or actions that form an identifiable pattern. Thinking you have a disease prevents you from being responsible for yourself. You can rationalize, 'I can't help myself.' I want you to know the answer is within, and so is the power to bring your life into balance."[7]

The five-step money management plan outlined in this book is one way to help bring balance to any area of spending abuse. Arenson's three-phase self-help program suggests first a financial examination[8] similar to the one outlined here in Step 3 which you're now reading about. Since I've been through it, I agree with

Arenson that the power to change patterns of debt-de-pendency resides within each of us. A budget helps be-cause it brings stability to an unstable financial environment.

Other Spending Evaluations

The Cost of Money Spent

We buy food because we need to eat. However, the kind of food we eat may determine our health and lon-gevity. Just as food purchased and consumed affects our physical well-being, how we spend money deter-mines our financial health.

Consider the cost of money spent without purpose. Suppose I have an interest-bearing checking account which earns approximately $25 per month. Each month when the interest is credited, however, I make no ac-counting for it so it is used for miscellaneous expendi-tures. The $25 simply disappears, and at the end of the month there is nothing to show for the expenditure.

Consider another alternative for using the $25 each month. Reinvest the earned interest in a no-load mutu-al fund which averages 12 percent return annually. In just 10 years a trivial amount of money becomes $5,751 if compounded monthly; 15 years will yield $12,490.

The same dynamic applies when we buy gadgets with little utility or spend significant amounts of mon-ey for fleeting pleasures. Using money with abandon not only dissipates the source but also prevents it from reproducing itself.

Compare the spending described above to a farm set-ting in times past. If a farmer uses all of the seed from his corn harvest, when planting time comes again, he will have no seed corn to plant to perpetuate corn production. One dollar spent rather than being invested at age 25 is equivalent to spending over $100 which would be available for retirement at age 65. The principle of reinvesting profits which help a business prosper also works for individuals and families. Reinvesting aids in establishing a strong foundation for a family.

Recreation Is a Valid Expenditure, Too

These illustrations help to establish a sensitivity to the real value of money we spend, not to imply that money should never be spent for recreation. Recreation is more than fun and games. Each of us is a unity— body, mind, and spirit—and there is an inner-relatedness of all our several qualities. We are whole persons; what affects the mind and body affects the spirit, and vice versa.

It is admirable to work hard and manage our money well. Providing for our families, being responsible citizens, and being charitable are all fine qualities. But all too soon we will burned out and be used up without some time and money used for renewal.

Recreation is the word *creation* with a prefix meaning "again" or "anew." The value of recreation is widely recognized. It is so important to physical and mental growth that school systems make it a mandatory part of their curricula from kindergarten through college. Corporations more and more are providing exercise equipment and allotting time for employees to work out because healthy people are more productive.

Becoming sensitive to how we spend our money may

reveal that not enough is being used for recreation rather than too much.

Balance Is the Ideal

It may sound as though I'm talking out of both sides of my mouth. (Don't spend your money; save and reinvest it so you'll have one hundred times more in retirement. But don't forget to spend some of your money for fun things.) Obviously, the ideal is a balance between the two. The ideal is to live a life with integrity.

Integrity is a good word to apply to all parts of our lives. It comes from the Latin *integritas* which means soundness, purity, or correctness. (The word *integer,* which we usually identify as a whole number, is a related word.) To live life with integrity means to be whole, intact, virtuous, honest, and blameless. That's a big order, but for a balanced life such virtues are worthy goals. Look at it this way. We all have room to grow.

Notes

1. Cecil A. Ray, *Living the Responsible Life* (Nashville: Stewardship Commission, SBC, 1992), 35. (Copyright: Convention Press, 1974. Revised and reprinted with permission. All rights reserved.)

2. Ibid., 35-36.

3. Ibid., 36.

4. George Barna, *What Americans Believe: An Annual Survey of Values and Religious Views in the United States* (Ventura, CA: Regal Books, 1991), 152-158.

5. Adapted from *Christian Money Management Workbook* (FS-1), (Published by the SBC Stewardship Commission, Nashville, TN, October 1991), 6.

6. Gloria Arenson, *Born to Spend: How to Overcome Compulsive Spending* (Blue Ridge Summit, PA: Tab Books, 1991), 9.

7. Ibid., 10.

8. Ibid., 76ff.

Your Plan for Financial Growth

"A family budget is a process of checks and balances; the checks wipe out the balance."[1]

—Arthur Langer

The formula for financial success can be reduced to two words: time and money. The younger you start, the less money you need.

There is nothing mysterious about how money grows. I have discovered that applying the growth formula is a rational process, and that ordinary people with even below-average incomes can be successful. Getting started only requires some simple, logical actions.

■ Eliminate consumer debt to increase buying power.

■ Forego some short-term, fleeting pleasures in order to achieve longer-term, more significant goals.

■ Establish a standard-of-living ceiling.

■ Develop a plan to manage income and expenses.

■ Conserve income growth.

■ Put money to work as well as working for money.

These are the actions I've used for 13 years to improve my financial strength. I only regret that I didn't start when I was younger. Not starting until age 40, I've had to be more diligent in order to reach an average level of financial stability than if I had started even five or ten years younger.

However, I'm relieved I did start, even at age 40. It's really never too late to begin. Even in retirement, this five-step plan can stabilize and improve your finances.

Step 4: Make a Plan for Spending

In the previous steps you have put together the building blocks of your plan for financial growth. Now it's time to start construction. The first part of this step is to compare income and expenses which you determined in the earlier steps.

INCOME AND EXPENSES COMPARISON (Based on information from Steps 2 and 3)		
Monthly Spendable Income	$	2,252.16
Less Monthly Expenses	— $	2,011.16
Undesignated Balance (+ or —)	+ $	241.00

Evaluate. If you have a zero or positive balance, you're in great shape for financial growth. But don't despair if you have a negative balance. There's nothing dishonorable about starting with a less than ideal budget. When Sarah and I started, we couldn't afford to designate money for gifts, miscellaneous expenses, or automobile replacement. Also, some of the necessary expense items could not be funded adequately.

One or more of the following solutions can help you either to eliminate a negative balance or to free more money for faster financial growth.

Solutions

Over the years I've used most of the solutions suggested here. The effectiveness of each suggestion will depend on your current life-style and financial status. As you read these ideas you may think of others that can help you improve your finances.

Attitude Retrofit

In years past *retrofit* was a word used to describe work done to make an older house more energy efficient. Used here, it means reprogramming your attitude about money and spending, if need be, to conserve financial resources.

Our attitudes about money and its use begin to take shape at a young age. Parents, other significant adults, and peers make potent contributions to our attitudes. I've observed that children often mimic the parent who is the primary manager in the home. However, some children rebel. Children who rebel may be responding to an exaggerated emphasis a parent places on money. Or children may rebel because of peer culture. Either way, imaging or rebelling, the parent still provides the impetus which shapes the child's attitude about money and which becomes the *modus operandi* when the child reaches adulthood. Retrofitting your attitude may help you and your children.

How do you change your attitude? The first step is to identify your attitude about money. Explore your past.

What is your earliest impression of the use of money? Was it used as a reward? Withheld as punishment? The primary contributor to your most pleasurable remembrances? A primary source of security? Or a measure of self-worth? All of these impressions can give money a power it doesn't deserve. Most are based on an emotional need created by a person or circumstance. Some of them were used as manipulation. Others are empty promises.

The second step toward changing your attitude is evaluation. If one or more of these or other impressions linger with you, compare your present feelings about money to them. Are your earliest impressions still driving your management and use of money? If so, move to the third step.

Three, retrofit your attitude toward money. It will take time, but teach yourself to respond to money in a more sound, sensible, unemotional way. Sometimes attitudes can be effectively changed by consciously substituting another attitude. For example, you might try memorizing a statement about money and recall it when reminded by occasions involving its use. Here's one example.

Money is a good and necessary commodity in our society, a medium of exchange, and nothing more.

Repeated enough times, it's possible to reprogram, retrofit, the way we think and react to money. I discovered that within a few months after starting our money-management plan I had shifted to a management attitude. Without consciously remembering, every use of money was evaluated by our management plan. A changed attitude about money and how we use it can help remove the emotional baggage attached to it and free us to manage it more wisely. No one or no other thing can determine your attitude without your permission.

Reduce Upkeep

Another possible way to improve finances is to eliminate some of the accumulated property which is not used enough to justify the money spent to keep it. We should also remind ourselves each time we contemplate another purchase that most products cost more than the retailer charges.

Glen and Sally Painter were newlyweds who had planned to wait awhile before starting their family. What they did want, however, was a dog. Shortly after their wedding they spent $300 for a registered puppy, using about half of their small savings. Soon after their purchase, the dog became ill. Within six weeks they owed their veterinarian over $600. Glen and Sally's $300 dog had become almost a $1,000 dog.

This dog story may seem like an extreme example, but it's true. True also is that what we buy costs more than the purchase price. When we buy a product it often must be cleaned, painted, repaired, or replaced. Each purchase becomes a liability. Referring to the encumbrance of material things, Thoreau wrote in *Walden* that people go through life "pushing all these things before them."[2] That is, with each additional item we accumulate, more money, more time, and more energy are required to use it and maintain it.

Look around. Are there one or more items you've acquired that are creating a financial drain, especially purchases seldom used? The financial drain may be caused by monthly payments which include interest charges, upkeep, taxes, registration fees, and insurance. It may be possible to eliminate the expense of a major item you enjoy but seldom use, such as a boat, motor home, or equipment, and rent the item when needed. The objective is simplification. As Thoreau also suggested, to the degree that we simplify our lives "the laws of the universe will appear less complex."[3]

There's a story about a typical middle-class family who moved near a devout Mennonite family. Observing all of the electrical appliances and equipment being unloaded by the movers, the Mennonite gentleman offered his counsel. "Neighbor, if you're missing anything or don't have room to get everything in the house, I'll be glad to show you how to do without it." Some simplification could greatly improve the drain on your resources, time, energy, and emotions.

Spending Habits

According to the philosopher writing in Ecclesiastes, "There is an appointed time for everything."[4] For many of the things we buy there is also a "best" time and/or place. With some planning, it's possible to pay less than regular price for most non-perishable products we buy.

● Need clothes—buy near the end of the season or at discount stores.
● Need heating/air conditioning—look for fall or spring sales.

● Need linens/towels—wait for February white sales.

● Need an automobile—shop December—February or the end of the month.

● Need household appliances—plan to buy during spring or fall sales.

Ideas for saving money are about as prolific as advice on how to rear children. We tend to become excited— maybe lose our heads—over sales. However, have you noticed, as I have, that most of the people with all of the good shopping ideas are no stronger financially than other consumers? There is a message somewhere in this observation. I've concluded that it's not as much when or where we buy as what we buy. I'm not saying when and where are unimportant consumer tips, merely not the most important.

The main problem is our impulsiveness. Over the years I've read several reports on consumers' spending habits. Most of the research indicates that between 60 and 70 percent of our decisions to purchase items are made impulsively. A recent report was about grocery shopping which estimated that 67 percent of purchases were made on impulse. Cutting coupons and buying sale items in the grocery store are worthwhile money-saving practices. But without meal-planning, which few people do, impulsive purchases effectively cancel out the other savings.

What is the solution? *Delayed buying response* is the label I've given to my family's practice of combating impulsive buying. When we started our money-management plan, Sarah and I agreed to stop and think before buying. No hard-and-fast rules were set. Rather, we consented that if we were doing planned shopping and discovered an item we had not intended to buy, we would walk away from it—not that we would refuse to buy it later, but provide time to evaluate whether or not we were responding on impulse.

This one shopping technique has saved us hundreds of dollars. Once I was tempted to buy a new radial arm saw costing about $400 plus sales tax. I walked away, examined my impulse to buy, evaluated my need, and determined that a used saw would serve my need just as well. Within two weeks I found a saw advertised in our local paper and bought it for $100, and didn't have to pay taxes on the purchase—about $330 saved by not buying the new saw. I could catalog a long list of similar experiences.

Credit Abuse

I've referred to and illustrated credit abuse several times. I believe the seriousness of the problem and the detrimental effects of credit misuse warrant the multiple references. Personal, corporate, and national debt has a stranglehold on people and the economy.

Our national debt is close to four trillion dollars. Just the interest payments on the national debt are over $292 billion. That's $17,000 indebtedness for every person in the United States.[5] In the months just prior to this writing, about half of the major airlines in the United States filed for bankruptcy and/or ceased operation. They couldn't handle their debt load when the economy turned down. What is true in the national and corporate world is also true with individuals and families. Bankruptcies are at an all-time high. Nearly one million people and businesses filed for bankruptcy in 1991.

The use of credit can have at least four detrimental consequences. As I've mentioned, it reduces buying power. If annual payments on consumer debt total $4,800 with an average interest rate of 18 percent, your buying power is reduced by $864 per year.

Second, if you regularly use a credit card for routine purchases, according to the banking industry, you will spend about 20 percent more than a person who makes cash purchases. It's psychological. When using a credit card, we don't give up anything; the credit card is returned after the purchase. Even writing a check rather than paying cash causes us to spend more, but not as much more as when credit is used. (The fact of increased spending when using credit also highlights the emotional attachment of the average person to money. That's another problem in another area which can hinder effective money management.)

Third, when debt ridden, a person or family is much more vulnerable during a poor economy and/or when employment is terminated. A person who has little or no debt is better able to make spending adjustments. After two or three years of effective money management and the accumulation of an adequate emergency fund, even unemployment can be managed for several weeks. An even stronger coping posture can be had by working toward paying off the house mortgage, too.

Fourth, for many people the continuous use of credit complicates careful planning. In fact, it may eliminate planning. By its nature, debt is a mortgage against future earnings. When, of necessity, keeping debt payments current becomes a consuming objective, that IS a person's plan for future spending. In cases of extreme credit abuse, the will to change is so diminished that survival is the only conceivable goal.

Reducing or eliminating debt is one of the more advantageous strategies to strengthen your financial base. Being debt-free can also put a charge in your self-esteem. Imagine the pride you can feel when shopping for an automobile and the sales person asks, "How do you want to finance it?" And you say, "I don't need financing; I pay cash!" After the purchase, you go to the courthouse to register your automobile, and when asked the name of the lien holder you smile and say, "There's not one." At the insurance company, the same exchange is repeated. It's a great feeling and a way to free money for more exciting goals.

Wise Use of Credit

Not all use of credit is bad. Occasionally, a situation will arise where credit is advantageous. When we included building a house in our goals, the first step was to find land. With no deadlines or pressure, we started looking for a building site. After about six months and sooner than we had anticipated, we found an excellent parcel of land and an opportune buying situation. The owner was facing foreclosure and was willing to sell 20 percent under market value. We didn't have enough money saved to pay cash. But having the purchase of land already in our budget, financing the balance needed was an expedient option.

Using credit to buy your primary residence is usually a wise use of credit. In most situations, buying a house is often a person's first and best investment. In the past 16 years and three houses later, inflation has increased my net worth over $80,000. That's more than $5,000 per year. Not a bad investment considering I was able to live in the houses, too.

However, buying a house may not be the best option in some circumstances. People who anticipate frequent relocation probably should find other investment options. Or, if owning a house in preparation for retirement is important, buy a house in a central location and lease it until needed. Also, when it's necessary to relocate in a less-populated area where resale would be difficult, even if you anticipate being there up to five years, buying a house may create financial difficulties later.

There are other wise uses of credit. I use a credit card for car rentals because of the insurance benefits provided with the card. Also, we all find ourselves in circumstances sometime when a service we must pay for is questionable. At such uncertain times I use a credit card if possible. I've found that if there's a problem with the service and/or the provider, with proper documentation the credit card company will remove the charge until the problem is resolved. The one time this has happened to me, the service provider did not pursue it, and I never had to pay for the improper service he had performed.

Using credit wisely can save money and increase your financial strength. However, using credit to buy sale items when cash is not available, particularly clothes, is seldom wise. Sales tend to exploit our weaknesses in managing money. When we use credit, we compound our weaknesses.

Develop Your Budget

You know your goals, income, and expenses. It's time to put your spending plan in writing.

Working with Your Bottom Line

If your income exceeds your expenses, you can immediately begin to fund some of your goals which are beyond ordinary living expenses—place more money each month into an emergency fund, eliminate consumer debt, fund an account to pay cash for automobiles, increase life insurance coverage, or begin investments.

If your expenses exceed your income, you now know by how much. Perhaps one of the solutions discussed above will provide a way to redirect expenses and bring income and expenses into balance. Or you may need to reduce your style and standard of living for a short time to get expenses under control. Whatever it takes, keep expenses from exceeding income. Let your goals for a brighter financial future become the driving force rather than succumbing to lethargy.

Goals Can Be Included and Achieved

You likely won't be able to include and fund all goals in your first budget, even if you have a positive balance. In fact, you may wonder if you can ever fund some of your goals considering your current financial status. Be patient. Time and management can accomplish miracles. If you're willing, here's how your goals can become realities.

Agree with yourself and, if married, spouses agree to establish a *standard of living line.* I know this is an imprecise art, but it worked for Sarah and me. Agree that you will live at whatever standard of living your current income will permit. Note that I said current income, not current standard which may be financed with credit. The objective is not to increase your standard of living as income increases. Believe me, this has been one of the most difficult money management commitments we've made.

By holding routine expenses at an established standard-of-living level, every increase in buying power frees money to begin building financial strength. This process can be illustrated graphically.

STANDARD OF LIVING LINE—
BUYING POWER INCREASES GRAPH

1	2	3	4	5	6
		Living Standard Line			
Income Now	First Raise	Pay off Debt	Second Raise	Third Raise	Interest Income

Here are some examples for using increases in buying power. With the first increase (column 2), if you begin with an imperfect budget, fortify—reinforce weak accounts, add accounts which could not be included at first. With the next increase (column 3), continue to strengthen or add accounts, especially an emergency fund. The next increase (column 4) might be used to fund an automobile replacement account. Subsequent increases (columns 5 and 6) could be used to start and strengthen investments or used for other goals according to priority.

Plan for Spending Allocations

Allocate a monthly dollar amount to each item in your budget. The expenses you recorded in Chapter 3 provide a starting place for completing your budget. Some expenses may need to be adjusted to keep your budget within the limits of your income. The total of all allocations should not exceed your monthly spendable income.

People spend money differently. Your budget is a personal document that includes expenditures which fit your life-style. Your spending will be different, even for common expense items, than that of someone else. And some of your expense items may be uniquely yours.

Remember, also, that one of the freedoms inherent in a budget is that you design it. No one dictates your expenses; you choose them. You determine how you want to live and spend your money within the limits of your income. That's responsible freedom which, based on history, provides the contentment most people search for in life.

PLAN FOR SPENDING[6]	
Account Items	Monthly Plan for Spending
1. Church gifts	$ 310.00
2. Home mortgage	580.00
3. Home insurance	
4. Home taxes	
5. Savings & emergency	60.00
6. Income taxes	
7. Social Security	
8. Retirement	
9. Life insurance	43.00
10. Health & accident insurance	
11. Hospital insurance	
12. Auto insurance	50.00
13. Loan payment	
14. Total other debts	75.00
15. Food	250.00
16. Clothing	75.00
17. Gas	
18. Electricity	90.00
19. Water	22.00
20. Telephone	35.00
21. Home improvements	
22. Home furnishings	32.00
23. Home maintenance	25.00
24. Auto repair	40.00
25. Auto gasoline & oil	70.00
26. Auto license	6.00

27. Medical & dental	40.00
28. Medications	20.00
29. Hospital	30.00
30. Subscriptions	3.00
31. School expenses	50.00
32. Cleaning, laundry	10.00
33. Allowances	20.00
34. Toiletries, cosmetics	10.00
35. Recreation, vacation	30.00
36. Gifts, birthday, weddings	20.00
37. Christmas	50.00
38. Auto Replacement	206.16
Total	**$ 2,252.16**

Income Allocations

After determining how much to designate each month for individual expense items, income needs to be distributed as received. If you receive income only once each month, and if your family has only one source of income received once per month, you don't need to complete the income allocations chart. Your plan for spending is your income distribution.

However, if you receive income twice or more per month or if your family has more than one income, allocations to account items must be made. An illustration may help you to better understand this process. In past years, an envelope system was suggested as a budgeting technique. When income was received, often in cash, it was divided for planned expenses by placing the appropriate amount of cash into a labeled envelope. For example, envelopes were labeled for house, food, clothes, utilities, etc. The envelope system was effective, but these days it's unwise to keep cash in your house.

Instead, deposit your income into a bank checking account and make the distribution on paper. The end result is the same, and using a bank provides greater safety for your money. The income allocation form has five columns. Each column represents an income period.

INCOME ALLOCATIONS[7]					
Account Items	Income Allocations				
	1	2	3	4	5
1. Church gifts	$115	$115	$ 40	$ 40	
2. Home mortgage	290	290			
3. Home insurance					
4. Home taxes					
5. Savings & emerg.		60			
6. Income taxes					
7. Social Security					
8. Retirement					
9. Life insurance		43			
10. Health & acc. ins.					
11. Hospital ins.					
12. Auto insurance			50		
13. Loan payment					
14. T'al other debts	75				
15. Food	125	125			
16. Clothing	55	20			
17. Gas					
18. Electricity			90		
19. Water			22		
20. Telephone			35		
21. Home imp'mts					
22. Home fur'gs				32	
23. Home maint.				25	

24. Auto repair		40			
25. Auto gas & oil	70				
26. Auto license				6	
27. Medical & dental			40		
28. Medications				20	
29. Hospital				30	
30. Subscriptions				3	
31. School expenses	50				
32. Cleaning				10	
33. Allowances	20				
34. Toiletries				10	
35. Rec., vacation				30	
36. Gifts, b'day				20	
37. Christmas		50			
38. Auto Replacement		57	49	100	
Totals	**800**	**800**	**326**	**326**	

Note: If income is received every two weeks, two months during a year you will receive three checks. If you receive income every week, you will receive five checks four months during the year, once each quarter. I suggest that regular, monthly, expense items—house payments, food, clothes, utilities, etc.—be funded with the regular two- or four-income periods each month. Use the two or four additional income periods each year to fund expenses which don't occur monthly—vacation, Christmas, some insurance, savings/investments, or maybe auto replacement.

When a family has two or more income sources each month, normally it's best to use separate income allocation columns for each income. For example, if both spouses have an income received twice each month, one spouse's income could be recorded in columns one and two and the other spouse's income recorded in columns three and four. (See illustration on chart above.) If one or both spouses are paid weekly, incomes can be combined or duplicate the allocation columns to accommodate the number of income periods needed each month—seven, ten, or more.

Tip: The amount of bookkeeping can be reduced by the way you record income allocations. Assume a two-income family paid twice monthly; therefore, there are four income allocations to be made. Using the medical and dental expense item to illustrate, assume a monthly spending allocation of $100. One way would be to allocate $25 each of the four income periods.

INCOME ALLOCATIONS					
Account Items	Income Allocations				
	1	2	3	4	5
27. Medical & dental	$ 25	$ 25	$ 25	$ 25	
28. Medications	$ 15	$ 15	$ 15	$ 15	
29. Hospital	$ 12	$ 12	$ 12	$ 12	
30. Subscriptions	$ 3	$ 3	$ 3	$ 3	
Totals	$	$	$	$	$

But bookkeeping can be reduced by using one income period to fund your medical and dental expenses in full—$100—while omitting other items. The next income period some of the omitted items can be funded in full. The 16 entries in the first illustration can be reduced to four entries.

INCOME ALLOCATIONS					
Account Items	Income Allocations				
	1	2	3	4	5
27. Medical & dental	$100				
28. Medications		$ 60			
29. Hospital			$ 48		
30. Subscriptions				$ 12	
Totals	$	$	$	$	$

Making income allocations may be the most tedious part of preparing a budget. But there's good news. Once you have completed your allocations, you will never need to repeat the entire process again as long as records are kept current. I made income allocations once 13 years ago, but only minor adjustments since. Now when I get an increase in income, only two or three item accounts need to be changed. The change takes five minutes or less.

Persevere! Muster your willpower! The rewards of preparing a budget that works and using it are certainly worth the effort. Over a period of 25 to 30 years it could be worth as much as a million dollars or more!

Notes

1. H. Arthur Langer, *Reader's Digest* (Nov. 1991), 35.

2. Henry David Thoreau, *Walden And Other Writings,* ed. Brooks Atkinson (New York: The Modern Library, nd), 3.

3. Ibid., 288.

4. Ecclesiastes 3:1 (NASB).

5. Paul Harvey, WKDA AM Radio, CNN Headline News, Nashville, TN, February 12, 1992.

6. Adapted from *Christian Money Management Workbook* (FS-1) published by the SBC Stewardship Commission, Nashville, TN, October 1991, 6.

7. Ibid.

Records: Keep on Track

For years at our house we frequently consulted the budget notebook. Now we keep our records on computer, but the printouts serve the same purpose as the budget notebook did.[1] The budget records encourage us and help us keep track of our progress toward goal-accomplishment.

Values of Record-keeping

If you have carefully completed the four previous steps, you have every right to feel a sense of accomplishment. Your work is essential in preparation for effective budgeting. But it's the record-keeping that provides the long-term dividends. Consider some of the more obvious values of keeping budget records current.

Guides Spending Decisions

One of the more useful purposes of budget records is decision-making. It seems that a lot of people decide to spend money based on the balance reflected in their checking account. (According to a recent news feature on CNN Headline News, 40 percent of U.S. citizens never balance their checkbooks. So they don't even have that reference point to guide their spending.)

For many years, I decided whether I could afford to buy some item based on my checkbook balance. Watching the checkbook balance may help us keep from bouncing checks at the bank, but it doesn't let us know if we can actually afford a particular purchase. When we use the checkbook balance to make buying judgments, it's difficult to anticipate the monthly fluctuations of money needed.

For example, in our pre-budgeting days, I tried to calculate mentally that the auto insurance was due in January and July; the family needed change-of-season clothes about April and September; my life-insurance-premium payment was due in May, ad infinitum. There is no way to keep all of the dates and dollar amounts needed in your head, and calculate how much money will be needed and when. Even trying robs us of creative mental energy and contentment. And, with no management plan, daily expenses usually demand the money before we ever come to seasonal needs.

How less taxing, simple, and effective to have current records from which intelligent spending decisions can be made! Suppose your checking account balance is $1,200 and you don't have an active budget. Your semi-annual auto insurance payment of $182 is due in four months. Do you know how much of your $1,200 bank balance is needed for auto insurance? Do you know if the $182 due in four months will be available when needed? With a glance at my budget records I can answer all such questions with absolute accuracy. This ability is freeing, fun, and fascinating.

Provides a Better Inheritance

Many parents have a compulsion to leave an inheritance of money to their children. This compulsion hasn't afflicted me as yet. It's not that I would mind leaving the children some money—rather I have discovered how to leave them something better. Teaching them how to manage is a better inheritance than money.

A family-management plan with an operating budget is a superb approach to teaching money management to children. Before our family had a budget, the children regularly asked Sarah and me for money when they wanted to buy something. The ritual is typical of most families with children, and a request often demands an immediate answer. One's mind rushes, trying to recall how much money there is in the bank. What other needs for money are pending? Then follows a quick mental evaluation of the priority of the child's request. In our pre-management days the answer frequently was, "We can't afford it."

After we set up our budget, when the children asked for money, the budget record book was consulted. The frustrations and questions that had previously accompanied such a request were practically eliminated. In fact, within a short time the children themselves were consulting the budget book and making some of their own financial decisions.

If a daughter wanted clothes, for example, she looked at the clothing-account balance in the book to discover how much money was available. If the clothing balance was sufficient to buy the item she wanted, she asked if it was OK. If there was an insufficient amount for the item of clothes desired, she went to Sarah or me and negotiated. "There's $45 in the clothing budget," she might report. "I need $60. Can I hold the $45 until Dad gets paid again and then use $60 for my clothes?"

Which exchange occurs around your house—the earlier description of my family or the latter one? Having a budget and teaching children how it works provides for them an inheritance better than money. The budgeting process also establishes family values that are passed on to children with the greatest of ease.

Promotes Healthy Discipline

I'm aware that most of us can make it without a written, active budget. Most people do. I know that if your income is average or above average and you regularly spend less than you earn, you don't have to allocate money to expense items and keep a current balance in order to pay obligations when due. But I also am aware that the use of a budget with up-to-date records is a healthy discipline. The joy and success I've experienced with money management has ushered discipline into my life in ways other than increasing my net worth. I'll illustrate with only two examples.

I'm much more sensitive to and disciplined about caring for the environment. Money management and ecology go hand-in-hand. When I conserve energy to improve my buying power, I help the environment. As I curbed my compulsion to spend on gadgets and fleeting pleasures, I saved money, cut energy consumption, and reduced pollution. My new sensitivity led me to become an active participant in recycling as soon as the opportunity was available. I am pleased with this new discipline in my life.

I feel even better about the discipline it has introduced into my Christian life. Various people will no doubt view this differently, but conscientiously managing my money is more in keeping with my understanding of Christian discipleship. Discipline and discipleship both come from the same Latin word *(discipulus)* which incorporates the ideas of "self-control" or "orderliness" and "learning."

As I've learned more about money management and disciplined myself to apply these principles, I have been able to enlarge my discipleship. The connection between money management and Christian discipleship is evident in the New Testament word *(oikonomos)*, translated *steward.* This is the Greek word from which we derive our English word *economics.* As I have pointed out before, the word *steward* in the Bible means "a manager of whatever God has provided." So, when I manage well the money God makes possible for me to earn, I'm practicing my discipleship. The better management also provides more money for me to use in Christian work. Money management and Christian discipleship go together like hand and glove.

Step 5: Keep Simple, Accurate Records

In the latter part of the previous chapter I explained how to distribute income to item accounts. I illustrated the process as making deposits into your bank checking account and dividing the deposits on paper to the item accounts of your budget. The illustration is even more explicit in this step. The form used to record deposits and expenditures for each item account looks like a checkbook register. In effect, the form for each item account is a sub-account of your main checking account at the bank.

Use a separate Item Account form for each category in your budget. The Item Account form to follow can be found in a larger size in the companion workbook.[2] You can reproduce that page for your use. Before putting my records on computer, I used a three-ring notebook with dividers labeled with the item-account names. The notebook provides room for multiple sheets of the item accounts you will use most frequently.

As few as 13 or 14 entries will be made on some item-accounts forms each year—one deposit each month and one or two expenses per year. Other accounts may have 20 or more entries per month—house and utilities, and maybe one other account where cash expenditures are most frequently recorded. When all lines are used on an item account sheet, add a new sheet on top of the old one and carry the balance forward.

ITEM ACCOUNT

Item Account Name _____   Monthly Plan for Spending $_____

| Income Allocation $_____ | Income Allocation $_____ | Income Allocation $_____ | Income Allocation $_____ |

Check No.	Date	Item Transactions	Deposits	With-drawals	Balance
Balance Forward from Previous Page					

Record-keeping

A Double-entry System

The design of this record-keeping process is a simple, double-entry system. Your checkbook register provides one entry and your budget book (or computer program) provides the other. When all deposits and checks are added and subtracted in your checkbook register, that's your balance. When those same deposits and checks are posted in your budget book, the total of all item accounts added together should equal the balance in your checkbook register.

There are other record-keeping systems, especially computer software programs. But many of them only help you keep up with expenses by the month. With the other systems, when you reach the end of the month, you can see precisely how much you missed your budget. The process suggested here provides a constant balance in the item accounts so spending decisions can be made any time the records are updated.

I keep my records current each week. Weekly posting seems frequent enough to make wise-spending decisions, but not so frequent that record-keeping becomes a nuisance.

Simplify, Simplify

An anonymous sage has noted that a budget will be used in direct proportion to its simplicity. I agree. For years before Sarah and I made a commitment to money management together and adopted our current budgeting process, I made up several. I enjoy detailed work, so I made budgets that were excessively specific. After a few weeks and usually no more than a month, each budget was abandoned. Why?

First, my budgets were one-sided, *my-sided.* The rest of the family, especially Sarah, didn't have input about what items were included and how much money was allotted to each item. A budget representing one family member's point of view will usually be ignored.

Second, a too-specific budget can defeat the best of us record-keepers. It might be interesting to know how much you spend on toothpaste each month, but you would be record-foolish to have a separate item account for toothpaste. In fact, the 38 item accounts I've used to illustrate Steps 3 and 4 are unnecessarily detailed for ongoing record-keeping. The same detailed item accounts in the previous steps, which help improve accuracy in setting up a budget, become a hindrance for record-keeping.

Simply! The 38 item accounts illustrated earlier can be reduced to 18 or fewer for record-keeping purposes. Make your budget as user-friendly as possible and still be able to monitor and control income and expenses.

SIMPLIFIED ITEM ACCOUNTS
FOR A WORKING BUDGET

1. Church/Mission Gifts
2. Home Mortgage/Utilities
3. Savings/Emergency
4. Insurance
5. Loans
6. Food/Toiletries
7. Clothing
8. Medical

9. Auto Repair
10. Auto Replacement
11. House Upkeep
12. Children
13. Recreation/Vacation
14. Gifts/Christmas
15. Wife-Personal
16. Husband-Personal
17. Charge Purchases
18. Miscellaneous

The work done in Steps 3 and 4 makes it possible to combine item accounts and still maintain control of spending with your budget. Take a look at the House Mortgage/Utilities account. After a dollar amount needed is established in Step 4 (Plan for Spending), several items may be combined for record-keeping. The separate item accounts for house and utilities budgeted per month might be:

House	$580
Electricity	90
Gas	40
Water	22
Telephone	35
Total Needed:	$767

As a combined item account, all house and utility payments can be recorded on one item-account sheet. The house payment/rent is a fixed expense usually recorded and paid in the same amount each month. It's an in-and-out item. What's left is for utilities. Since electricity and/or gas usually have the largest seasonal fluctuations, dollar accumulations in low- demand periods (spring and fall) will be for larger expenses needed in high-demand periods (summer and winter).

Similar simplification can be made in other budget areas that logically can be combined. However, I suggest that budget items with the potential of getting out of control be kept separate—food and clothes, for example. Though I have not found it necessary to separate merchandise normally bought at a grocery store— food, household cleaning supplies, toothpaste—I've found it helpful not to combine this general category with others.

If a week before the next income is received the food (grocery store) account is about depleted, wise management would suggest conservation of food. It's still possible to prepare nutritious yet inexpensive meals on a reduced budget. If you end a month and have overspent an account, tighten up on expenses for that account to catch up. Wise management includes controlled distribution of both money and the products we buy with money. Should you end a month with money left over in the food account, don't splurge. Remember that when you have guests, particularly during holidays, it will require more money for food. It's good to accumulate some surplus funds.

Tips for Getting Started and Record-keeping

Cheat Your Way Out of a Hole

A frequent question I hear from people attending my conferences is, "How do I get started?" They understand the wisdom of management and the process I've presented. What they can't figure out is how they're going to change their cycle of just "living from one paycheck to the next."

Most people's income is sufficient to set up a theoretical budget on paper. Income distributions can be made (Step 4), but when they start using their budget they can't seem to get out of the hole. They need to pay the house mortgage (rent) before enough money can be accumulated. Or they realize that a six-months auto-insurance premium is due in two months, which means they're four months in the red from the beginning. Their first thought is, *I need a month's income or more ahead just to get my accounts started. How can I ever catch up?*

This is reality and the price that must be paid for past mismanagement. I don't have to remind you that I experienced the same dilemma when I started budgeting. With no guidelines to follow, I simply did what I had to do to make my budget work. What I did is the only solution I've ever discovered. You "cheat your way out of the hole." I'll illustrate what must be done.

Of course, the need is for more money to help you progress. With the same income, the only way to free up money is to cut expenses. In our case, we agreed to a moratorium on spending for most flexible expenses. Our first month, for example, we spent only about $100 for food, a savings of $150 of the $250 budgeted.

No clothes were bought for about three months, another $100 saved each month. Fortunately, we had to use only a small amount of the money we budgeted for medical expenses, so another $40 was accumulated. Other item accounts accumulated a balance because of reduced spending, but these are sufficient for my illustration.

Assume a mortgage payment of $580 is due on the first day of the month. But to make an equitable distribution of income to budget accounts, only $290 can be allocated for the house payment from the first-of-the-month income. The other $290 needed will not be available until the fifteenth of the month. Yet, the mortgage must be paid the first of the month. Here's what to do.

Pay the mortgage, $580, and show a negative balance on the account of -$290. The fifteenth of the month $290 more will be deposited and posted to the account leaving a zero balance. In the meantime, money allocated to other item accounts is not being used. Remember the spending moratorium? At the end of the first month, transfer the following amounts from other accounts to the mortgage account (you're cheating on your budget):

From	To Mortgage Account
Food account	$150
Clothes account	100
Medical account	40
	$290

With these transfers, the mortgage account ends the month with a $290 balance. When income is received the first of the second month, another $290 will be posted to the mortgage account, and the monthly payment can be made without creating a negative balance.

If there is another account requiring a large payment each month, it may be necessary to follow the same procedure for another month or two. In fact, the illustration above of catching up the mortgage payment could be extended to two or three months if the amount is too much for one month.

The mortgage account is now on-line. In the future, when the mortgage payment is due the money will be available. After all of your accounts are on-line, the cheating should stop. As you resume normal spending, what is budgeted for each item account must not be used for other expenses.

Note also in this example that net worth has grown $290 the first month as a result of reduced spending. That's significant progress for one month. With managed spending, when interest payments are mostly eliminated, and hopefully with some occasional increases in income, buying power and net worth will steadily increase.

An Easy Way to Manage Cash Expenditures

How often I've said and heard others say, "When I have cash in my pocket, it just vanishes." Without an easy method of knowing what cash is being spent, it does feel like it's evaporating. Most people are like me in that they refuse to keep up with every penny of cash they spend. So how can cash be managed without carrying around pencil and paper to record every cash expenditure?

I've discovered a method that works for Sarah and me. Maybe it will be helpful to you, too. Earlier in this chapter I illustrated how to reduce the number of item accounts for record-keeping purposes. In that list are two item accounts—wife-personal and husband-personal. In our budget most cash expenditures are from these two accounts and require little additional record-keeping.

My philosophy of cash management in a personal budget is to shape the budget around the typical pattern of spending. That is, when setting up your budget, include in one or two item accounts most of the purchases for which you use cash. When cash is withdrawn from your checking account, you record the withdrawal as one expenditure with little or no additional record-keeping required. Purchases made with cash are budgeted in the item account from which the withdrawal is subtracted in your budget. Here's how it works in our budget.

One item account in our budget is called Lee/Personal and another, Sarah/Personal. The monthly amount of money set aside for these item accounts (Step 4) is determined by the kinds of purchases we routinely make. Each of our item accounts include:

Gasoline for the car each drives
Snacks, etc.
Hair care
Personal toiletries

Small, miscellaneous personal items

When I withdraw $50 from our checking account for pocket money, I subtract the $50 from my personal item account as though it were already spent. As long as I'm spending the cash for the items listed above, I don't need to keep additional records of my spending. I seldom, if ever, overspend the amount allocated for my item account because I know what the money will be spent for.

However, I do make a few cash purchases which are not budgeted in my personal-item account. When I make such purchases, I keep the receipt or make a note of the expenditure. For example, at least once each week I stop by the store to buy needed food items-- milk, bread, etc.—and pay with cash. At the end of the week when I "do our books," I transfer the amount of cash I spent for food to my personal-item account.

On the food-item account, I record the expenditure just like I would record a check written for food. The line on the food-item account form might look like this:

FOOD ITEM ACCOUNT					
Check No.	Date	Transactions	Deposits	With- drawals	Bal.
Balance Forward from Previous Page					83.60
Trans	3/18	To Lee/personal		10.50	73.10

After the food expenditure has been recorded, and to complete the transaction, I turn to my personal-item account and make a similar entry, except that it's shown as a deposit instead of a withdrawal.

LEE/PERSONAL ITEM ACCOUNT						
Check No.	Date	Transactions	Deposits	With- drawals	Bal.
Balance Forward from Previous Page						42.20
Trans	3/18	From food	10.50		52.70

(When the computer software program designed for this record-keeping system is used, only one entry is necessary. If, for example, I pull up the Lee/Personal-Item Account, I show a deposit and designate the Food-Item Account as the source. The computer program makes the deposit to my personal item account, records the same information on the Food-Item Account as a withdrawal, and updates the balance on both item accounts.)

The Personal-Item Accounts are not limited to cash purchases. If a check is written for something budgeted in a Personal-Item Account, it is subtracted as it would be for any other item account.

Managing Charge Purchases

Managing charge purchases with this record-keeping system is similar to managing cash purchases. It begins with an assumption that all expenses have been included in the budget and any charged purchases made will be paid in full each month. If you begin your budget with outstanding charge accounts due to be paid off, include those charges in your Loan-Item Account. Any new charge purchases should be subtracted from the appropriate item account and transferred to a Charge-Purchases-Item Account as a deposit. The Charge-Purchases Item Account becomes a holding account, retaining the money until the bills come due. Then, when the credit-card statement for the previous month arrives, pay the bill and subtract the check from the holding account.

For instance, you charged a clothes purchase. At the end of the week enter a transfer on the Clothes-Item Account and subtract the amount of the charge purchase. On the Charge-Purchases-Item Account enter a transfer and show it as an addition. When the credit-card bill is due, the money needed to pay it will be in the Charge-Purchases-Item Account.

Managing Reimbursed Business Expenses

For those of us who are reimbursed for business expenses, a record-keeping procedure similar to managing charge purchases can be used. A Business-Travel-Item account can be included in your personal budget so personal and business expenses can be kept separate. Depending on how you're reimbursed for business expenses, this item account may regularly have a zero or negative balance. I'll illustrate with my business travel.

On a typical business trip I will charge expenses on my personal bank card (motel or rental car) and make cash expenditures (usually food). When I have completed the trip, I turn in an expense report along with receipts to the business office. In the meantime, I need to account for cash and charge expenditures in my personal records.

The money for cash expenditures on the business trip came from the Lee/Personal-Item account in my budget. So I make a transfer of funds from the Business- Travel-Item Account to my Personal-Item Account to replace the cash I spent on the business trip. For charge expenses I transfer funds from the Business-Travel-Item Account to my Charge-Purchases-Item account. (Now, stay with me. It's not at all difficult!) These transfers almost always create a negative balance in my Business-Travel-Item Account until I'm reimbursed.

When reimbursed for business expenses, I deposit the check in my bank checking account and record the deposit in my Business-Travel-Item account. If all of my records have been accurately recorded, the balance in my Business-Travel-Item Account will be zero.

Why maintain such detailed records? It keeps balances in Personal-Item Accounts accurate for sound spending decisions at all times by all family members. It assures that money for charge payments will be available when needed to avoid paying interest.

Living in a Tension

The 5-step plan for wiser money management I've described, along with the record-keeping system, has been a delightful experience for Sarah and me. You have probably figured out, though, that it hasn't been without tension along the way. I sometimes bump into a form of Christian tradition, and people holding to that tradition, who would detract from the joy we've experienced. It's the issue of having faith versus planning and working toward future goals.

Confronting the Detractors

Some Christian traditions renounce well-defined goals that can keep us on track and challenged. Notice I used the word "traditions," not Christianity. One Christian tradition tends to frown on personal assertiveness and achievement. It's usually not overt, but subtle. It teaches a form of unbiblical meekness and dependence in a manner that may breed lethargy. "Just have faith, and God will take care of you."

I've staked my life on faith in Christ, and the promise that God will take care of me and mine, but I don't understand that to mean I'm supposed to be completely passive. Be on guard when tradition insinuates that it's A-OK to be average—maybe even better to be poor—or suggests that we not excel too much because it may look as though we're not depending on God.

That's so different from the challenge of the Christian message. Meekness in the Bible is controlled strength. "Blessed are the meek: for they shall inherit the earth" (Matt. 5:5). Dependence on God is for strength to achieve. The thrust of the Christian message is growth—be on your way to becoming a mature, finished personality, conformed to God's image (Matt. 5:48).

The Bible is filled with goals for the believer that require controlled assertiveness and personal achievement, as well as an abiding faith. *I would be the first to affirm that a person can never manage money to the extent he/she can escape the need for God's care and provisions.*

Joy in the Midst of Tension

I've named many benefits, particularly in the introduction, you can derive from consistent money management. There are, no doubt, other advantages I could list, and even the ones named will have different meanings for different persons. But our family has received one joy far more significant than some of the benefits I've listed.

One of our goals I didn't list in Chapter 1 illustrates how setting goals and Christian faith can be merged. When Sarah and I made the commitment to money management, we did so out of Christian conviction. Sarah wanted to do volunteer mission work. This specific goal may not interest you, and it would apply only to Christians, but it illustrates how a commitment to money management can reshape and redirect the future.

Personal involvement in mission work excites Sarah. At the time we started our money-management plan, there were hundreds of refugees coming into our city. Sarah longed to reach them with Christian concern, especially to teach them English, but she lacked time and money.

Our money-management plan helped solved both problems. Sarah resigned from her job, which gave her the time, and we allocated $35 each month for her literacy-mission work with the refugees. Her ministry with those immigrants was successful and personally rewarding to her. Some of those first refugee families are now our personal, Christian friends and well-adjusted, productive American citizens.

Other fascinating results ensued because we chose to include this goal in our plans. An almost insignificant monetary goal of $35 per month mushroomed into a life-changing experience. As involvement with the refugees increased, Sarah gained experience and acquired more literacy training. Soon she was a qualified literacy trainer, teaching others to do literacy work. Her involvement also resulted in four literacy-mission trips to Burkina Faso, West Africa, for a total of 15 weeks and one trip to Peru. When we first established our financial plan, we could not have imagined the doors our goals were going to open.

Our simple goal to provide for Sarah's volunteer mission work continues to amaze us with its expansion. As a result of her mission involvement, since 1986 she has been director of an inner-city mission center. Together, Sarah full-time and I part-time minister through our church where the center is located.

It fascinates me how wise money management can make life more challenging and delightful. This one seemingly small financial goal has reshaped the last half of our lives and has determined what we will likely do during our retirement years. As noted earlier, we plan to be involved in long-term foreign mission projects.

You, no doubt, will face tensions when finances are reshaped to accomplish goals you've chosen. But when you encounter detractors, remember the old adage: you can't guide a ship unless it's moving. It seems to me that God can use people who are on the move more than those who are dead in the water.

Notes

1. *The Christian Manager* is a computer program based on the five steps discussed in this book. It is for IBM and compatible computers and requires 512 kb of RAM. Order from SBC Stewardship Commission, 901 Commerce Street, Suite 650, Nashville, TN 37203-3634, or call 615/244-2303.

2. *The Christian Money Management Workbook* can be ordered from SBC Stewardship Services, 127 Ninth Ave. N., Nashville, TN 37234 or call 1-800-458-2772.

Appendix

Information in this appendix is in addition to the steps discussed in the previous five chapters. All of the appendix material is related, but I still want to keep the five steps in focus. Some or all of this material may be helpful at different stages of your money- management pilgrimage. Review the headings or scan the contents to determine what will be helpful to you now or in the future. I particularly encourage you to review the section on insurance.

How to Balance Your Checkbook

CNN Headline News Radio reported the results of a survey of adults in the United States.[1] According to the survey, 40 percent never balance their checkbook. From personal observation, I also know that many adults have never spent time learning how. Yet, basic to effective money management is record-keeping, including the use of a checking account. And your checking account needs to be kept in balance—your checkbook register balanced with your bank statement each month. In terms simple enough for a child to understand, here's how it's done. (I suggest you also teach your children how to balance a checkbook. More than likely no one else will teach them.)

Your Checkbook Register

When you deposit money into your checking account, the bank adds the amount deposited to the balance in your account. When you write a check and it arrives at your bank, the bank subtracts the amount of the check from the balance in your account. (I told you I was going to make it simple.) Your checkbook register illustrates this process, if you faithfully record each transaction.

CHECK REGISTER

Check No.	Date	Checks Issued To or Deposit Received From	Deposits	✓	Check Amount	Balance
		Balance Forward from Previous Page				1218.21
586	11/29	Department Store (clothes)		✓	38.41	1179.80
X	11/30	Deposit (salary)	1500.00	✓		2679.80
587	12/1	Mortgage Company (house pmt)		✓	680.00	1999.80
588	12/1	Food Store		✓	63.29	1936.51
X	12/4	Interest (on checking account)	6.75			1943.26
X	12/6	Deposit (return on medical ins)	82.92			2026.18
589	12/7	Electric Company			101.67	1924.51

The first column of the register is the check number which corresponds to the checks written. Check numbers are copied from each check, usually located in the upper right-hand corner of your checks. Each check has a different number. The date column is, of course, the date you write checks or make deposits. The "To" and "From" columns remind you to whom the checks were written and note the reason for each check and/or the source of the money you deposit. This information is vital for your record-keeping.

The "Deposits" column is for recording the dollar amount of deposits, and the "Check Amount" column, for the amount of checks written. The column with the check marks is used when balancing your checkbook and will be discussed later. The last column is where the remaining amount or "balance" in your checking account is recorded. Deposits are added to this column, and the amount of each check written is subtracted.

Reconciling or "Balancing" Your Checkbook with Your Bank Statement

You should balance your checkbook each month soon after you receive your statement from the bank. Otherwise, correcting errors the bank might have made may not be possible. My bank allows 60 days for errors to be reported and corrected.

Your bank statement shows all deposits you made and checks you wrote the previous month, provided they reached the bank's accounting department before the statement was printed. Your statement will also show your account balance at the beginning of the statement period and your account balance as of the date the statement was printed. On the back of your statement there will usually be a form to use to balance your checkbook with the bank's statement of your account. It may look similar to the one illustrated here, except that it will have no figures on it. (Refer to the "Check Register" illustration above and the "Reconciliation Form" which follows as you to read.)

RECONCILIATION FORM			
To Help You Balance Your Bank Statement			
Month November 19			
Checks Outstanding No.	Amount	Bank's Ending Balance (From this statement)	$ 1950.01
589	101.67	Add Deposits (Not shown on this statement) Total (+)	$ 82.92
		Subtract Checks Outstanding (Total from left) (−)	$ 101.67
		BALANCE	$ 1931.26
		Balance In Your Checkbook	$ 1924.51
		Add (Interest, Credits not shown in checkbook) (+)	$ 6.75
		Subtract (Service charges, drafts, other charges) (−)	$ 0
		BALANCE	$ 1931.26
TOTAL	$ 101.67	The two BALANCES should agree	

The first thing to do when you receive your bank statement is to compare the deposits you have recorded in your checkbook register with those shown on your bank statement. Place a check in your checkbook register by each deposit which is also shown on your bank statement. If a deposit was made, for instance, after the day the statement was printed, it won't be shown on your bank statement, but you will have it recorded in your checkbook register. Don't mark that deposit in your checkbook register and write the amount on the line of the "Reconciliation Form" that instructs you to "Add Deposits (not shown on this statement)."

Next, compare the checks you have written and

those the bank has listed on your statement with your checkbook register. In your register, place a check mark by each check you wrote which has cleared the bank and has been recorded on your statement. Checks you have written but not shown on your bank statement should not be marked. (That's why the bank balance is sometimes more than your checkbook balance. Those checks will be listed on next month's statement.) The checks you didn't mark should be recorded on the "Reconciliation Form" in the "Checks Outstanding" section.

Look at the "Reconciliation Form" illustration. One check for $101.67 has not reached the bank. A deposit of $82.92 was made two days after the bank statement was printed and is not shown. Notice that beside the section to record and add "Checks Outstanding" there are two sections for reconciling your bank statement with your checkbook register. The top section begins with the bank's ending balance and the bottom section, with the balance in your checkbook register. When both sections are completed, the ending balance of each section should agree as in the illustration.

If, after studying this example, you don't understand the process completely, ask someone to help you. Maintaining a balanced account is important for your ongoing money management.

Insurance Needs

This sounds so simplistic but . . . everything you do revolves around your life. If you die or are disabled, the most valuable asset you have is lost or diminished. So, the head of a household should protect his or her most valuable asset with insurance, particularly where there is a spouse and/or children involved.

Also, wise money management includes protecting your other vulnerable and important physical assets. There are four significant kinds of insurance to include in your protection program—life insurance, medical insurance, disability insurance, and property and liability insurance.

Life Insurance

AMOUNT OF LIFE INSURANCE NEEDED (For Head of Household)	
1. Cash Needed Immediately by Family Survivors	(Example)
(Estimate costs for funeral, unpaid medical expenses, debt payments including house mortgage, relocation of family, and children's and/or spouse's additional education.)	$ 100,000.00
2. Ongoing Annual Income Needed for Survivors	
(Determine annual salary needed to live comfortably then subtract benefits which will be available such as Social Security survivor benefits, pension plan benefits, etc. The result will be the additional annual income needed.)	$ 4,000.00
3. Money Available From Estate for Investing	
(Add face value of all existing life insurance policies, savings, stocks, bonds, income-producing assets, etc. These are the total assets family survivors can invest and receive income.)	$ 72,000.00
4. Amount of Additional Life Insurance Needed	
(Add the amount of money needed for family's immediate cash needs, line 1, and the amount of money for family to invest to earn the ongoing income needed, line 2. Then subtract existing assets, line 3. The total estimated additional life insurance needed for the head of the household is:)	$ 68,000.00

(Add the amount of money needed for family's immediate cash needs, line 1, and the amount of money for family to invest to earn the ongoing income needed, line 2. Then subtract existing assets, line 3. The total estimated additional life insurance needed for the head of the household is: **$ 68,000.00**).

Life insurance is usually for the benefit of family members left after a person's death. Life insurance creates an immediate estate and compensates for the loss of earning power of the person who dies. So, with some accuracy you can estimate the amount of life insurance needed. There are basically three kinds of life insurance: whole or straight life, universal, and term. Whole life provides protection, accumulates cash value, and has a level premium throughout one's lifetime. Whole life has the highest premiums of the three kinds until about age 65.

Universal life is essentially level-term insurance with an investment instrument. It provides protection and has a level premium. Part of the premium pays for protection, and the rest is invested in an annuity or other interest-bearing instruments. Universal life is usually less expensive than whole life but more expensive than term insurance.

Term insurance comes in several varieties. With level term, the premiums are fixed for a set period of time—usually ten or more years. Guaranteed-renewal term can be annual renewed or renewed in five-or-more year blocks. Premiums usually increase annually. Decreasing term has a level premium, but the face value of the insurance policy decreases each year.

Guaranteed-renewal term is the best buy of the three major kinds—whole life, universal, and term. This kind is especially wise for young families with children who need much more life insurance on the head of the household than older families. Also, with wise money management, as a family's net worth increases the need for life insurance drops proportionately.

Medical Insurance

Providing medical insurance for a family requires a much larger percentage of spendable income now than in years past. However, successful money management requires it. Families are vulnerable when it comes to medical expenses, and without insurance families can easily be financially crippled for years, if not for a lifetime.

There are not many ways to reduce the cost of medical insurance. Group plans are usually less expensive than individual. For people who are not covered by an employer's group plan, there may be other kinds of groups you can qualify for—farmers, small businesses, trade groups, etc.

If you simply cannot afford full coverage, you may be able to provide major medical for your family. A major- medical plan begins to pay a percentage (often 80 percent) after you have spent a defined amount for an illness or accident (maybe $1,000 or $2,000).

Disability Insurance

Disability insurance is important protection many people overlook. According to statistics, we are more likely to become disabled during our working years than to die or be killed prematurely. In addition to loss of income, disability often creates a continuing financial drain because of the medical treatment needed. Young families especially need disability insurance.

Disability insurance is usually much less expensive than life insurance. Costs can be reduced further by increasing the amount of time between the disability and the time the insurance begins to pay monthly benefits. For example, disability insurance that begins to pay 30 days after a disability costs more than a plan that begins to pay after 90 days. By practicing wise money management and establishing an emergency fund, you can choose the 90-day plan. Disability insurance is typically coordinated with Social Security or other benefits and is keyed to a percentage of income at the time of disability.

Property and Liability Insurance

Property and liability insurance are combined into one policy. The two most common types of combination policies are also the two most needed by individuals and families—homeowners insurance and automobile insurance.

Homeowners (Renters) Insurance.—There usually are three levels of homeowners insurance—HO-1, 2, and 3. The HO-1 provides the least protection and HO-3 provides the most. Your insurance company can provide information about the differences of coverage. Generally HO-3 coverage is not that much more expensive and is the best buy of the three levels of coverage.

When buying homeowners insurance (or a similar

policy for renters), look for a policy that increases coverage automatically because of inflation, sometimes called "value up." Likewise, choose a policy which replaces contents at current costs, not one which pays for items at their "used" value.

Homeowners insurance is better than specific kinds of insurance such as fire and storm because it includes liability and medical coverage. The liability and medical coverage protects you in case someone has an accident on your property and/or sues you. Also, should you have rental property, for which you can't buy homeowners insurance, you can usually add liability coverage for the rental property to your homeowners policy on the house in which you live.

There are circumstances in which you may need additional property insurance or at least a supplement added to your homeowners policy. Flood insurance is one example. Another example is expensive items or heirlooms. If you have jewelry, for instance, which exceeds the dollar limit of your basic policy, you will need to obtain additional coverage.

Another circumstance not covered by homeowners insurance is equipment used in business. Business equipment is usually defined as any equipment you use to generate income. If you have a computer that is utilized for writing personal letters, keeping your own records, or used for games, it probably will be covered by your homeowners insurance. However, if you use that same computer to do contract work for which you are paid, the computer is classified as business equipment. The same classifications apply to mechanic's tools, woodworking equipment, etc. If used for a hobby, they are usually covered; but if used to generate income, they will be classified as business equipment.

Automobile insurance.—It's dangerous financially to drive an automobile without insurance. Similar to homeowners insurance, automobile insurance can include property damage, medical, and liability as well as other coverages.

The comprehensive and collision part of your insurance covers your automobile. There are two ways to keep cost of insurance down in this area. First, the higher your deductible the less the cost. The typical deductible is $100. However, if you raise the deductible to $250 or $500, it costs less. Second, after an automobile depreciates below about $2000, if you have your finances in order, you may want to drop the comprehensive and collision altogether.

The liability part of your automobile insurance protects you against personal and property damage to others, including your passengers. Most states require a minimum of liability, some as low as $10,000. These days $10,000 is not nearly enough. Liability should probably be a minimum of $300,000, which doesn't cost much more than a lesser amount which may be required.

There are several other kinds of coverage that can be included in your automobile-insurance policy. Medical insurance for yourself and family can be included. The value of this type of insurance is questionable if you are covered by another health-insurance plan. If so, you're probably paying for double coverage since multiple medical insurance plans usually are coordinated.

Uninsured motorists and road service can also be included in your automobile insurance. Uninsured-motorists provision depends somewhat on laws of your state. Some states require insurance carriers to provide it as a part of the basic policy. If the laws of your state do not protect you otherwise, by all means include uninsured motorists in your policy. Unless you drive extensively, road-service coverage probably is not worth the cost to provide it.

When It's Time to Invest

Investing money is altogether appropriate if done in a timely and responsible manner. By timely I mean investing after other essential financial plans are in place and adequately funded. The three primary plans that precede investing for financial growth are a well-planned and working budget, an emergency fund equal to at least three months of spendable income, and adequate insurance coverage. One of these, the emergency fund, has some relationship to investing but distinct from investing for rapid growth or for retirement.

Responsible investing refers to the level of risk taken and the ethics of the companies in which one invests. Some forms of investments seem to be so risky that Christians should not participate.

Then there are the ethical issues: For what is the invested money used? Does it fund industry, research, and products that are of questionable moral value? Is the money invested used for the benefit of society? Are the corporations, etc., using the invested money in a manner that negatively impacts the environment? Most of these questions can be answered with a little research. In fact, there are mutual funds which are moral-, ethical-, and environmental-specific. They specifically avoid the immoral and the unethical and concentrate on environmentally friendly issues.

Investing Emergency Money

Your emergency money should be reasonably accessible, normally available at least within a few hours if needed. However, it can still be invested so you may keep up with or exceed the inflation rate. Your emergency money should not be left in a no-interest account. The minimum expectation would be a passbook-savings-account rate.

Money-market funds usually pay more interest than passbook savings and are accessible instantly. Usually you can write a specific number of checks each month in minimum amounts. (Three checks per month with a $250-per-check minimum is an example.) Because of more interest and check-writing privileges, a money-market account for emergency money is usually an advisable choice.

I can think of at least one exception, that could have several twists to it, where emergency money would not need to be accessible within a few hours. If, for instance, interest rates on certificates of deposit (CDs) are higher than normal, and if a line of credit could be established with the CDs as collateral, you might justify investing in CDs with maturities of six months or more. The possible drawback is the cost of setting up the line of credit and a possible annual fee if the line of credit is not used.

After you put your money-management plan in

place and functioning, you can investigate your alternatives. The pressing goal is to work toward having an adequate emergency fund.

Investing for Net Growth

Probably the first and best investment a person or family can make is to buy a house to live in. A house is one of the few investments people can make, use, and enjoy at the same time. There are some exceptions to the wisdom of buying a house. For people who must relocate frequently, buying a house to live in (that must be sold when relocation is required), can create problems. This problem is compounded if it's necessary to move into a less-populated community where resale of a house is made even more difficult.

After investing in a house, the next level for most people is preparing for retirement income. An important consideration when investing for retirement is tax sheltering and tax reduction. Using the tax laws to your advantage can increase the earning power of your money as well as creating an estate that will nurture you in retirement.

Excellent methods are available to help you reduce taxes and make your money grow tax deferred for retirement. For wage earners eligible for 401(k), 403(b), or Keogh retirement plans, both income taxes and Social Security taxes can be deferred on income contributed to these accounts. Further, interest accumulated on invested funds is not taxed until the money is withdrawn. Deferred taxes on deposits and earnings means faster growth of retirement funds because there can be 30 to 45 percent more money available to invest and thus earn interest.

There are limits and restrictions on these accounts, and you will need to learn about them, but these types of accounts are among the best investment strategies available. Generally up to 20 percent of income can be placed in the 401(k) and 403(b) plans. More can be put in the Keogh plan. If you qualify for any of these accounts, generally it's advisable to shelter the maximum amount possible before considering other types of investments.

An Individual Retirement Account (IRA) is another retirement planning strategy. The amount of money that can be placed in an IRA each year is usually less than the 401(k), 403(b), and Keogh plans, and there are restrictions on who can participate. However, if an IRA is all you qualify for, it's still better than other investments that offer no tax shelter at all. You will pay Social Security on money placed in an IRA, but income tax is deferred if you are under the income limit. Even if you are over the income limit to qualify for income-tax deferment on the front end, interest will still compound tax deferred until withdrawn after age 59½.

My choice of investments for self-directed IRAs and investments, in addition to tax-sheltered retirement plans, are no-load mutual funds. There are hundreds of mutual funds available, so it will require some research to determine which one(s) is(are) best for you. But the search can be intriguing and rewarding.

Mutual funds are made up of many stocks and/or bonds and other types of investments. Fund managers have an objective and follow a predetermined strategy about which kinds of stocks, bonds, etc., they will invest fund money in. When you place money in mutual funds, you buy shares in the funds. Just as individual stocks, share price is determined by the market performance. The difference in mutual funds and individual stocks is that mutual funds are made up of many different stocks, bonds, etc., which comprise the funds' portfolio. As do many individual stocks, many of the mutual funds also pay dividends.

Diversification is the reason mutual funds have become ideal investment vehicles for the average person. For example, it's unwise to place all of your investment money into one stock, even if it's a solid one. The possibility of something going wrong is ever present. But for the small investor, buying shares in many different stocks would be difficult and time-consuming. With mutual funds a manager of the funds provides the diversification for you. They are so much more in touch with financial markets that their decisions can be more informed than yours or mine.

Mutual funds come in all shapes, sizes, and kinds. Generally they fall into four categories labeled by different terms. Conservative funds invest in such instruments as money-market securities and U.S.-government-money funds. The risk of losing money invested is highly unlikely. The conservative funds typically have a lower rate of return. For safety, the conservative funds often are recommended for people near retirement and after retirement. The rate of return is usually better than passbook savings and CDs, and nearly as secure.

Moderately conservative funds also invest in guaranteed government securities but also include high-

grade common stock and bonds. The moderate categories of mutual funds usually focus on producing income. They, too, can be a vigorous instrument for investing funds near and past retirement. They are
slightly less secure than conservative funds but have a
higher rate of return.

Moderately aggressive and aggressive funds focus on
capital growth with income secondary. As you would
guess, they are progressively less secure but also offer
greater opportunities to increase the rate of return. Aggressive funds are typically recommended for younger
investors. The prevailing philosophy is that unlike older investors, younger people have time to recover from
a loss—thus, more risk with the potential for greater
return is a valid approach.

Aggressive funds are typically recommended for investors to age 50 or slightly beyond. However, it's usually smart to have a small percentage of retirement
money in aggressive funds up to and even beyond retirement to help counter inflation. At mid-50, I have
one IRA in a moderately conservative fund and one in
an aggressive fund. The aggressive fund investment is
less than 10 percent of my retirement money pool.

How can you educate yourself more about investing,
particularly in mutual funds? Begin by looking at the
business section of your newspaper where mutual
funds are listed. Notice that in the "Sell" column oppo-
site the name of the funds some have a NL for "no-
load." That means the fund does not charge a percentage of money invested for commission when fund
shares are purchased. Too, the fund normally does not
have a back-end charge when shares are sold. If a fund

does have a back-end charge, it will be footnoted in the financial magazines and in the prospectus for the fund.

You may also become familiar with mutual funds by reading financial magazines. Your public library likely will have one or more of these magazines. The two I read monthly are *Money* and *Kiplinger's Personal Finance* magazine. Every month both magazines have one or more sections on top-performing mutual funds that usually list performance for one, three, five, and ten years. Also, each year both magazines ordinarily list several hundred of the mutual funds ranked according to their performance for the past year. Almost monthly the magazines will have feature articles on some aspect of mutual funds.

Other information about mutual funds to be found in magazines is their category, grade, and the telephone number to call to request a prospectus. In the magazines, no-load funds are identified under the column titled "% Maximum Sales Fee" as "none." The prospectus is where you find out what types of businesses, etc., the fund invests in. The prospectus also provides a financial statement of the fund and past performance.

Mutual funds are not the kind of investments that you use to "play" the stock market. You can move in and out of funds as often as you care to, but the prevailing philosophy about mutual funds is to select one which has a good track record and stay with it for at least five years. Obviously, there are exceptions. If a fund begins to consistently perform poorly, then a move sooner would be in order. You will understand as you begin to read about mutual funds.

Wills and Funerals

Wills and funerals may be difficult for some people to talk about. But let's face reality: none of us is going to live forever (on this earth), so why not do the "decent thing" for our families and protect our estates at the same time? For Christians, these preparations are more than a "decent thing" for our families; they are a reflection of our Christian commitment and responsible stewardship.

Your Will[2]

A will drawn up according to the laws of your state of residence is a valuable part of your financial planning. First of all, your state has already prepared a will for you, just in case you never get around to it.

Take my word, you probably won't like the will your state has so graciously provided. The state's will does provide some consideration for your family, but they also protect their interests. And the state's will is not too concerned about conserving your estate and making the best use of it. The only way to override the state's will for you is to prepare one of your own.

A properly drawn will can be a comprehensive, written legal description for the distribution of your real and personal property. The distribution can be to family members, Christian causes, charities, etc., some of which the state's will does not provide. When your family is young, your will should probably concentrate on provisions for the family. This is especially true when minor children are involved. In your will, you can name a guardian for your dependent children. Husband

and wife will likely want to make reciprocal wills and name each other as guardian. But each will should also name an alternate guardian in the event both parents die in a common accident.

Your will is used to name the executor of your estate. In reciprocal wills, each spouse can name the other; but as with the guardian, an alternate executor should be named. This executor does not have to be the guardian of your children. To be completely sure of having someone responsible for your estate, you should also name a co-executor. The co-executor could be an institution such as a foundation or bank trust department whose continuing existence doesn't depend upon one person.

Your will should undergo several revisions during your lifetime. There is wisdom in reviewing it annually, even if you're not aware of a need for changes. But at each change in your family's life cycle it needs to be revised—when children are born, reach maturity, marry, become disabled, or when parents become disabled or die. Changes in vocation, income, real and personal property, retirement, a spouse's death, and other events also signal the need to revise your will. A move to another state creates an urgent need to revise your will because state laws differ so widely.

Funerals

Some people have joked, "I can't afford to die. It costs too much." Funerals can cost loads of money, but they probably will cost much less if you make some preparation.

It's extremely thoughtful for a person to put in writing wishes concerning his or her funeral. Such instructions can be attached to your will as a letter of last instructions. It's not legally binding, but it's certainly emotionally fortifying for the family members left after death. Last instructions can include the place for the memorial service, the officiant and order of service, and the place of burial. Some of these preparations can physically be arranged beforehand—for example, the burial site. The advisability of such prearrangement depends on your mobility and the place a family can agree on to call home.

The most important point I want to make about funerals is costs. If prior arrangements have not been made by the deceased, decisions for the funeral must be made by family members under extreme emotional duress. Often the wisest decisions are not made financially. Gripped by a sense of profound loss, family members' first impulse may be to provide the most lavish accoutrements—the best casket, vault, flowers, and arrangements. Thousands of unnecessary dollars can be spent on a funeral.

I suggest one of two procedures. Either prepurchase the casket and vault, if that's possible, or put in writing the quality of the items and services to be purchased. I'm not as much suggesting less expensive as opposed to more expensive, but a price range consistent with the size of the estate left by the deceased. Personally I have difficulty justifying the most expensive items, no matter the size of the estate. For example, what needed advantage does the most expensive vault offer compared to the least expensive. Both keep the dirt on the grave site from caving in, which is what the law usually requires. How important is it that the expensive vault is guaranteed not to leak for 100 years and the less expensive one is not?

I was reminded recently of another financial concern families should consider when a member of their family dies. Unjustified medical expenses could be charged to the family when any of the deceased's organs are donated for transplantation or for medical research. This concern is not directly related to the funeral itself, but the expenses could not occur unless the person dies.

Both of the two possible scenarios place tremendous pressure on the family members. The first case is a situation where an accident victim or the family of the victim wishes to donate organs. In order to preserve the organs to be transplanted, it's possible to keep a brain-dead person alive many days artificially waiting for the right transplant situation. Who pays for these days of the most expensive kind of intensive medical care?

You can see immediately the pressure on the family. Is there a chance of recovery? Who decides, the physician in charge or the family? And this scenario would also question the ethics and integrity of one or more physicians. Such a situation is so case-specific I wouldn't attempt to offer a solution. I would encourage families to talk about such an eventuality. A living will might help relieve some of a family's responsibility.

The second scenario logically follows the first. Who pays for the removal of organs to be transplanted or used for science? We would assume the person or laboratory receiving the organs. I'm told our assumption might not be true. This situation is easier than the first one. A careful check of the final medical bills and some hard questions may provide the needed information. Attention to details could save thousands of dollars needed by a family after the death of a family member.

Teaching Your Children How to Manage Money

Impressions children acquire about money last a lifetime. People generally have a similar attitude about money at retirement age as they did at the time they became young adults. Helping your children, then, learn how to manage money is especially valuable. It's a responsibility also swaying other emotional- and social-growth processes.

Christian parents have an added incentive for helping their children learn to manage money. Managing money is one essential element of Christian commitment; excellent guidance by parents will enhance most expressions of children's faith.

Parents have many approaches to influencing and informing their children about money management through normal child-rearing experiences.

Basic Training

According to psychoanalytic theory, children's first impressions about money likely begin to develop during their second and third years. This is the stage when most personality patterns develop. These will have long-lasting effects on people's lives. It seems that clear concepts about money will begin to develop at about five years of age.

It is important to help children build a sense of self-worth not related to material things (Matt. 6:19-20).

Having personal property is not wrong. The problem of accumulating wealth is in identifying one's self-worth and security with one's wealth. That's why most people absolutely come to pieces when their property is lost, stolen, or destroyed.

Security is in relationships, not things. When parents overemphasize accumulation of material wealth, they reflect an insecurity that is then passed on to their children. In contrast, biblical teachings focus on security in relationships, with God through Christ and with other Christian people. Parents' expressions of faith in how they manage money is one of the best examples of security they can hand down to their children. By investing in people and Christian ministries, parents teach their children they can have security and self-worth *because* of a personal relationship with Christ, not in material "baubles, bangles, and beads."

Children should also be taught to view money objectively, not emotionally. Teaching children objectively is accomplished by not using money as either a punishment or reward. The purpose of money is to meet needs. Using money any other way gives it a power it should not be allowed. If children are taught to attach an emotional value to money, future money management decisions can be distorted.

To guide their children's basic training in money management, parents will want to be aware of how children learn. They "pick up" attitudes about money and habits in the use of money. Questions can be used to evaluate attitudes and habits.

Do your children often hear you fight over money? If so, they likely will conclude that money is charged with negative emotions. What about your heritage of attitudes and uses of money? When you were a child, was money used for any purpose other than meeting needs, purposes such as expressing love or a way of punishment? Does having money heighten your sense of power over other people? Does associating with poor or rich people make you uncomfortable?

Hands-on Experience

Managers are made, not born. That's why it's necessary for parents to give their children hands-on experience. Children's experiences can include involvement with their parent's money management and managing their own money.

Before age five or six, children have difficulty understanding the relative value of money. Give them a choice between a dollar bill and a quarter, and they likely will choose the quarter; it's more appealing to their senses. Also, they have little or no concept of planning ahead, an essential element of money management.

By the time children enter the first grade, though, they usually know that 50 cents will buy more than 25 cents. What they need are experiences to help them make life-style choices about quality and quantity and planning beyond the present moment.

With younger children, arrange for them to shop for small personal items you normally buy for them. Suppose a six year old needs two or three items for school. On entering the store with your child, determine how much the items will cost in the appropriate quantity for the situation—for example, paper in a 100-count package instead of 500-count. Give your child enough money to pay for the purchase, guide his or her choice of the right quantities by explaining the quantity-price difference, and then let the child pay for the items.

There are at least three immediate values to planned shopping with children. It teaches them that money is to be exchanged for what people need. Guiding young children's shopping helps them learn to make wise decisions about quantity and later about quality. The first two experiences help develop the third, that of learning to plan ahead.

By age five or six, children can usually manage a small allowance received once or twice per week. Allowances are an excellent way to give children hands-on experience in managing money without much investment or risk-taking.

The basic principle for providing a child an allowance is freedom. An allowance should be for the child to manage. Parents can establish the ground rules on the front end, what necessary expenses are to be expected from the allowance. But for a child to learn to manage money, there must be freedom to make mistakes.

The amount of an allowance should match the child's maturity. Too much or too little of an allowance frustrates a child. Too much allowance with too much responsibility for a child's age usually means that the lessons learned are too costly. Or the child is taught to spend irresponsibly. Too little allowance for a child's maturity may cause the child to be overly dependent on his or her parents or lose interest in trying to manage the little bit of allowance received.

Allowances for younger children are for inexpensive, personal things. From age 8 to 10, allowances can include necessary personal expenses such as school supplies and a child's gifts to the church. Older children's allowances also can include some clothing items.

Dispense allowances regularly. For children 6 to 9 or 10 years of age, it's best to give allowances once each week. After about age 10 children should be encouraged to plan for at least two weeks. Older children can plan for a full month.

Suggesting regular allowances also means giving the allowance at about the same time each week or month, similar to receiving income from a job. Providing regular allowances does at least two things. It prevents a child from having to ask for money, making it appear that getting money is a hassle to be expected. Second, the regular time becomes a reference point for children. They can hold parents accountable. Also, parents can hold children accountable, in the event the allowance is asked for early.

Timing can be important to a child's good money management. Consider dispensing allowances near bedtime rather than during a shopping trip. Given when a child cannot spend the money immediately, there's more time for planning, and thus better management.

An allowance should be a child's share of the family's income, not pay for doing certain chores. Conversely, a child should be expected to perform assigned tasks within the family because he or she is a part of the family. Failure to perform a task should not be punished by withholding the child's allowance. This form of punishment has two possible negative side-effects. It can cause a child to assign unwanted emotional value to money; the person dispensing money has power over other people. Also, withholding money becomes equal to withholding love; love and money are confused.

However, it's not inappropriate to pay a child for work if the same work would normally be contracted to someone outside of the family. Just be sure that clear guidelines are established beforehand.

The place of an allowance often is confused when a child begins to earn money. Should the allowance be discontinued, continued but reduced, or continued as usual? Ideally, the allowance should be continued for the reasons cited above; the child is a part of the family. However, if a family has inadequate income or a child desires independence, the allowance could be reduced or discontinued. Just be sure all family members share in the sacrifices.

If a child wants independence, clear guidelines should be established about what parents will pay for and what the child will provide. Also, because a child begins to earn his or her own money doesn't mean parents forfeit their responsibility to teach money management. Earning their own money doesn't automatically qualify children to make wise management decisions.

In fact, working children may need more guidance. In addition to money management, they must also manage their time. Children who want to work usually are well motivated, and they may want to work too many hours. Five to 20 hours of work per week, depending on the child's age and academic level, should be acceptable. More than 20 hours weekly is counterproductive.

Parents' Commitment

The value of the parents' guidance in developing good money-management practices in their children has been referred to several times; it's absolutely necessary. In reality, there's a prior step that informs parents' guidance. Christian parents need to commit themselves to biblical principles of money management. Becoming knowledgeable of and applying Christian management principles in their own lives qualifies parents to help their children learn to manage money.

Notes

1. WKDA AM Radio, CNN Headline News, Nashville, TN, December 30, 1991.

2. Adapted from: Lee E. Davis, *In Charge: Managing Money for Christian Living* (Nashville: Broadman Press, 1984), 150-152.